Small Business Web Sites

Made EASY

Steven Holzner

New York Chicago San Francisco
Lisbon London Madrid Mexico City
Milan New Delhi San Juan
Seoul Singapore Sydney Toronto

The **McGraw·Hill** Companies

Cataloging-in-Publication Data is on file with the Library of Congress

McGraw-Hill books are available at special quantity discounts to use as premiums and sales promotions, or for use in corporate training programs. To contact a special sales representative, please visit the Contact Us page at www.mhprofessional.com.

Small Business Web Sites Made Easy

1234567890 DOC DOC 019

ISBN   978-0-07-161481-8
MHID   0-07-161481-8

Sponsoring Editor	**Acquisitions Coordinators**	**Proofreader**	**Illustration**
Roger Stewart	Carly Stapleton	Paul Tyler	Lyssa Wald
Editorial Supervisor	Joya Anthony	**Indexer**	**Art Director, Cover**
Janet Walden	**Technical Editor**	Jack Lewis	Jeff Weeks
Project Editor	Richard Mansfield	**Production Supervisor**	**Cover Designer**
Emilia Thiuri	**Copy Editor**	Jean Bodeaux	Jeff Weeks
	Jan Jue	**Composition**	
		Dodie Shoemaker	

To Nancy, of course.

About the Author

Steven Holzner is a Web entrepreneur whose business has been consistently very successful. He's also the award-winning author of over 100 books in 18 languages, and has been a contributing editor at *PC Magazine*, as well as being on the faculty of Cornell University and MIT.

About the Technical Editor

Richard Mansfield has written 41 books, mostly on computer topics. He is a recognized expert on teaching programming to beginners. Overall, Richard's books have sold more than 600,000 copies worldwide, and have been translated into 12 languages.

Contents at a Glance

Introduction

Welcome to our book on creating business web sites. So often when you read about creating business web sites, you read about marketing, email lists, and shopping carts, but nothing about the actual mechanics of building your site. Or when you read a book about creating web sites, there's nothing focusing on business per se.

This is the book that changes all that. This book focuses on both the mechanics of building your site and the business side as well. You'll find all you need for a good working knowledge of building business web sites, from soup to nuts.

What's in This Book

This book is crammed with information, from start to finish. Here's an overview, chapter by chapter.

Chapter 1   Essential HTML   This chapter gives you a guided tour of HTML, from the very basics up to the intermediate level. This chapter serves as an introduction and reference for HTML, the foundation of any web page.

Chapter 2   HTML Tricks   This chapter is all about HTML tricks designed to give you an edge. From the basics, such as using frames, to more advanced techniques, such as using Dynamic HTML, you'll find a smorgasbord of powerful HTML effects here: creating image maps, using links to creating navigation bars, updating text on the fly, drawing logos, downloading images on the fly, creating visual effects, setting element visibility, and XHTML. This chapter will boost your web pages from ordinary to extraordinary.

Chapter 3   Optimizing Cascading Style Sheets   As of HTML 4.0, you're now supposed to use Cascading Style Sheets to customize all aspects of your web pages' visuals, from underlining text to positioning items in your pages. This chapter gives you all you need.

Chapter 4   Powering Up with JavaScript   JavaScript makes your page come alive in the user's browser. The number of things you can do with JavaScript is unlimited—snazzy mouseovers, downloading data behind the scenes without browser refreshes (Ajax), opening new windows, creating flyout menus, updating targeted parts of the browser window, using cookies, blanking text fields when they're clicked, making the browser navigate back to its previously opened window (just like the browser back button), validating data before it's sent to the server—all this and more is possible. You're going to get a good overview in this chapter.

Chapter 5   Site Design and Search Engine Optimization   This chapter discusses business web site design and search engine optimization (SEO). After you finish this chapter, you'll have a good working knowledge of both topics.

Chapter 6   Marketing   This chapter covers Internet marketing. Here, you're going to learn all about pay-per-click advertising, free advertising, email lists, hit meters, and more. Getting the word out there is essential if you want customers to come to your site.

Chapter 7   Marketing on Facebook   Social networking sites have been gathering a lot of attention these days because of their overwhelming popularity, and their young demographic, which is very tempting to marketers. This chapter covers the most promising of the social networking sites for marketers—Facebook.

Chapter 8 Server-side Power: PHP   In this chapter and the next, we're going to take a look at working with PHP on the server. Most ISPs now offer support for PHP, and you can do very powerful things with it. You can save data in files on the server (such as guestbooks); interact with SQL databases; accept and read user input in HTML controls like text fields and check boxes; set and read cookies; and even draw graphics on the server (such as an interactive stock chart) and send them back to the browser.

Chapter 9   PHP: Cookies, Sessions, Browsers, and More   In this chapter, you'll turn PHP loose and push the envelope. Cookies, sessions, drawing images on the server, determining the browser type, and more—it's all here.

Chapter 10   Taking Credit Cards Online   In this chapter, you're going to take a look at the good part of online stores—getting the money. You'll learn how to get a merchant account, set up your own shopping cart, use shopping cart software, use online store-creation software, PayPal, Google Checkout, and more.

It's all coming up, so turn to Chapter 1 now and dig in.

Essential HTML

Welcome to your guided tour of creating your own business site. From this book, you will get a real working knowledge of how to create attractive business sites from start to finish.

That's not to say we can cover the entire topic here—these days, that would take a 20-volume set of books. But this book is truly designed to give you all you need to get a strong business site up and running, and to start interacting with customers. You'll find dozens of professional-level skills in this book, ranging from creating a basic page all the way to accepting credit cards.

Some companies have millions to spend on their site and years of programming time to invest. We'll assume that you have neither. Rather than costly web page solutions (hiring professionals to do the whole job for you), everything we'll use in this book is free and designed to let you build sites that give you a solid, healthy web presence.

Some Business Sites

Let's start off by taking a look at some business web sites that are already out there. A couple of the businesses we'll take a look at depend on the Web for their very livelihood, so you know they emphasize their web pages.

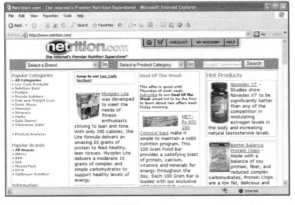

Figure 1-1   The netrition.com web site

We'll start with a nutrition site—and one of my favorites—netrition.com, which you see in Figure 1-1.

I like netrition.com for their products, but not so much for their web site design. Take a look at Figure 1-1—the site is overcrowded, packed with information and text. It doesn't provide an easy entry point that draws customers in. Sure, you can use the site—it's not difficult—but it does involve a little learning curve. And you don't want to make customers have to think to use your site.

Next, take a look at ebay.com in Figure 1-2. eBay obviously depends on its web site for its very existence.

However, that's not a great site either. While netrition suffers from too much density, too many elements vying for your attention, eBay's site suffers

Figure 1-2   The ebay.com web site

from the opposite—it is too diffuse, without any central focal points. Your eye roves over the page, looking for something to focus on.

Now take a look at usatoday.com, which appears in Figure 1-3.

This page is much better composed. There's an immediate focal point in the large text, "Housing starts still weak," which draws the eye in. The titles below it are in smaller type, and the eye, once attracted to the leader text, easily scans down the other titles.

Providing a good focus as usatoday.com does is

Figure 1-3   The usatoday.com web site

Figure 1-4   The amazon.com web site

a very important aspect of business page design—you want to draw the user in and to make it easy to access your site. This book emphasizes clean design with strong focal points.

Take another look at Figures 1-1 to 1-3. All those start web pages lead into very complex sites filled with dozens or even hundreds of pages. Note that such depth and complexity aren't readily apparent in those start pages. Instead, they all use menu bars or drop-down lists of links to let users easily navigate to where they want. In other words, how the user is able to navigate your site is very important, and your site's organization should allow for easy navigation. In addition to clean web pages with accessible focal points, this book will also stress easy and self-evident navigation.

One of the best sites for navigation is amazon.com, which you can see in Figure 1-4.

Amazon.com is a huge web site with hundreds of thousands of pages, and organizing that took some thought. As you can see in Figure 1-4, Amazon's solution was to provide menus of links with submenus. Rather than showing all they've got in 200 links up front, they tuck them away to be easily accessed by the user.

Let's look at the page we'll create in this chapter; it's just a basic page, but it will illustrate and review how to work with HTML.

Creating a Web Page

I assume you're not a total beginner when it comes to HTML. I don't assume much HTML knowledge, and we'll go through a review here. But if you're totally at sea in this chapter, it's a good idea to take a look at a book on HTML before proceeding.

3

Hundreds of HTML editors will enable you to create your own HTML pages. A partial list of HTML editors appears in Table 1-1.

Amaya	Aptana	Arachnophilia	Blaze Composer
Bluefish	CoffeeCup HTML Editor	Contribute	Dreamweaver
Evrsoft First Page	FrontPage	Freeway	GoLive
HomeSite	HTML-Kit	KompoZer	Microsoft Expression Web
Mozilla Composer	Nvu	Quanta Plus	RapidWeaver
SeaMonkey Composer	Serif WebPlus	TrellianWebPage	Virtual Mechanics SiteSpinner
WebCreator	Website X5	Web Studio	

Table 1-1   Some HTML Editors

Table 1-1 doesn't even take into account the hundreds of proprietary HTML editors that the major web hosting companies such as 1 & 1 have for their customers' use.

If you want to use an HTML editor, by all means do so. However, I believe it's essential that you also have a working knowledge of HTML. Sooner or later (usually sooner), you'll get results from any HTML editor that are not what you want, and you'll have to go in and fix things. To do that, you'll have to know HTML; it's not hard. For that reason—and because everybody's favorite HTML editor is different—we're going to cover some in-depth HMTL in this and the next chapter.

If you have a favorite HTML editor, please feel free to keep working with it. But you'll also want to know how to work with HTML by hand when you start adding JavaScript to your pages in Chapter 4, or when you want to connect to

Figure 1-5   Our sample HTML page, top half

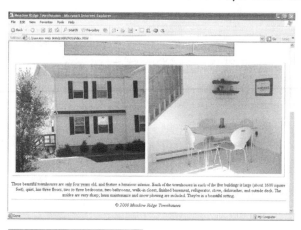

Figure 1-6   Our sample HTML page, bottom half

server-side scripts, as we'll do in Chapter 8.

To get up to speed on HTML, we'll build the simple web page you see in Figures 1-5 (top half) and 1-6 (bottom half).

This web page is a mockup of a business site for Meadow Ridge Townhouses, and it's not very fancy—but it does give Meadow Ridge Townhouses a presence on the Web, and it gives viewers of the page a way to contact the company (through the e-mail link you see in Figure 1-5).

Note that this page has a strong visual focus, as you can see in Figure 1-5. The page is not very cluttered, and the photo of the townhouse building you see at top and center attracts the eye. There aren't a lot of conflicting elements vying for your visual attention, and the result is that the page draws the user in (although the bottom two photos are a little too big—it's usually better to surround your images with more whitespace).

This web page is named *index.html,* because that's the default name browsers look for when the user navigates to a web site. In other words, this is the page that will come up by default if the user just navigates to www.meadowridgetownhouses .com. For reference, here's what index.html looks like. If you understand everything here, feel free to skim the following discussion where we dissect it:

```
<html>
  <head>
    <title>
      Meadow Ridge Townhouses
    </title>
  </head>

  <body bgcolor="#fffff5">
```

5

6

```
<center>
  <h1><i><u>Welcome to Meadow Ridge Townhouses</u></i></h1>
  Send us email at <a  href =
    "mailto:info@meadowridgetownhouses.com?subject=Rentals">
    info@meadowridgetownhouses.com</a>!
  <br>
  <br>
  <img src="triplex.jpg" width="600" height="339"
    border="1" alt="townhouse">
  <br>
  <br>
  <table border="1" cellspacing="8">
    <tr>
      <td><img src="side.jpg" width="461" height="383"
        alt="side"></td>
      <td><img src ="chairs.jpg" width="476" height="384"
        alt="chairs"></td>
    </tr>
  </table>
  <br>
  These beautiful townhouses are only four years old, and feature
  a luxurious interior. Each of the townhouses in each of the
  five buildings is large (about 1600 square feet), quiet, has
  three floors, two to three bedrooms, two bathrooms, walk-in
  closet, finished basement, refrigerator, stove, dishwasher,
  and outside deck. The insides are very sharp; lawn maintenance
  and snow plowing are included. They're in a beautiful setting.
  <br>
</center>
<hr>
<center><i>&copy; 2008 Meadow Ridge Townhouses</i></center>
</body>
</html>
```

MEMO

The World Wide Web Consortium are the people in charge of HTML, and you can find them at www. w3c.org. If you ever have questions about what's legal in HTML and what's not, take a look at the W3C site for the definitive answer. Later in this chapter, you'll see how to *validate* (that is, check the syntax of) HTML pages using the W3C site.

Now that we've seen index.html at work, let's take it apart. To follow along, you only have to use a text editor to create this page, such as the free Notepad or WordPad editors that come with Windows. Just make sure you save the HTML page in plain text format. The default for WordPad is RTF (Rich Text Format), which browsers can't use. To save a document as plain text in WordPad, select

File | Save As, and then, in the Save As Type box, select Text Document. Also make sure that the filename extension is *.htm* or *.html*; save this example page as **Index.html**.

Starting a Web Page: <html>

HTML stands for "Hypertext Markup Language," and the "markup" part of that refers to everything in angle brackets (< and >). That markup gives directions to the browser on how you want to display the web page. For example, you use the b *element* to indicate that text should be bold, like this: `<b>This text is bold!</b>`. An element consists of an opening *tag*, `<b>` here, and a closing tag, `</b>` in this case.

Elements can contain other elements (child elements) inside their opening and closing tags, and may also have *attributes*, which are given in *name=value* pairs in an element's opening tag, like this in the body element's opening tag: `<body bgcolor="#fffff5">` (the name of the attribute here is bgcolor, and its value is `"#fffff5"`). Technically, you don't have to enclose attribute values in quotation marks to let your HTML be read by a browser, but we will do so because it's listed as a requirement by the World Wide Web Consortium (W3C), and it's a good practice. It's also strictly required in HTML's cousin, XML.

All elements and text in an HTML page must be enclosed inside an html element, so we begin index.html with that element:

```
<html>
      .
      .
      .
</html>
```

All other elements and text in the page are enclosed in the html element, such as the page's head, coming up next.

7

Creating a Web Page Head: <head>

A web page's head is where you place certain data about the page, such as
its title (which will appear in the title bar of the web browser). The head
section of a web page is enclosed in the head element, which is a child of
the html element:

```
<html>
  <head>
    .
    .
    .
  </head>
    .
    .
    .
</html>
```

The head element is supposed to contain a title element (which the W3C
says is required for all HTML pages, although browsers won't have a problem
if you omit it), and that's coming up next. Besides the title element, head
sections can contain other data, such as meta elements, which provide
information about the page for search engines (which we'll take a look at in
Chapter 5), Cascading Style Sheets (Chapter 3), and script elements to place
JavaScript in the page (Chapter 4).

Adding a Web Page Title: <title>

The title element encloses text that you want to have appear in the browser's
title bar, such as the text "Meadow Ridge Townhouses" in our sample page:

```
<html>
  <head>
    <title>
      Meadow Ridge Townhouses
    </title>
```

```
        </head>
          .
          .
          .
    </html>
```

Besides appearing in a browser's title bar (see Figure 1-5), the title is one place to put keywords you want search engines to find your page with—more on this in Chapter 5.

Next up comes the web page's body, where most of the action is.

Creating a Web Page's Body: <body>

The body element comes after the head element and contains all the display elements of the web page:

```
<html>
  <head>
    <title>
      Meadow Ridge Townhouses
    </title>
  </head>

  <body bgcolor="#fffff5">
          .
          .
          .

  </body>
</html>
```

The body element contains the text and images that appear in web pages. Note the use of the bgcolor attribute, which sets the background color of the web page. As with most HTML elements, the body element supports numerous legal attributes. Here's the list for the body element:

■ **alink**   Color of hyperlinks as they're being clicked. Set it to a color value or predefined color name.

■ **background**   The URL of a graphic file to be used for the browser's background. This is usually a simple, pale texture that, if smaller than the page, is automatically tiled by the browser.

■ **bgcolor**   The color of the browser's background. Set it to one of the predefined colors or a color value.

■ **bgproperties**   Indicates if the background should scroll when the text does. If you set it to FIXED, the only allowed value, the background will not scroll when the text does.

■ **bottommargin**   Specifies in pixels the bottom margin, the empty space at the bottom of the document.

■ **class**   The class of the element (used for rendering).

■ **dir**   Gives the direction of directionally neutral text (text that doesn't have an inherent direction in which you should read it). Possible values: LTR: Left-to-right text or table, and RTL: Right-to-left text or table.

■ **id**   A unique alphanumeric identifier for the tag, which you can use to refer to it.

■ **lang**   Base language used for the tag.

■ **language**   Scripting language used for the tag.

■ **leftmargin**   Specifies the left margin, the empty space at left of the document, in pixels.

■ **link**   The color of hyperlinks that have not yet been visited (as far as the browser keeps track). Set it to a color value or predefined color name.

■ **marginheight**   Gives the height of the margins at the top and bottom of the page, in pixels.

■ **marginwidth**   Gives the width of the left and right margins of the page, in pixels.

■ **rightmargin**   Specifies the right margin, the empty space to the right of the document, in pixels.

■ **scroll**   Specifies whether a vertical scroll bar appears at right of the document; can be `Yes` (the default) or `No`.

■ **style**   An inline style indicating how to render the element.

■ **text**   The color of the text in the document; set it to a color value or a predefined color.

■ **title**   Holds additional information (as might be displayed in tool tips) about the element.

■ **topmargin**   Specifies the top margin, the empty space at the top of the document, in pixels.

■ **vlink**   The color of hyperlinks that have been visited (as far as the browser keeps track). Set it to a color value or predefined color name.

Note that we're assigning the `bgcolor` attribute, which sets the background color of the page to `"#fffff5"`. That's a *hexadecimal color triplet*, which is how you specify colors in HTML. Color triplets work like this: `"#rrggbb"`, where `rr` is the red value, `gg` the green value, and `bb` the blue value. Each value is expressed as a two-digit hexadecimal number, from 00 to ff (in decimal, that's 0 to 255).

Want an easy way to create color values? Look at a color picker, such as the one at http://www .pagetutor.com/colorpicker/index.html, which you see in Figure 1-7. If you see a color you like, you can let the mouse cursor rest over it, and its color

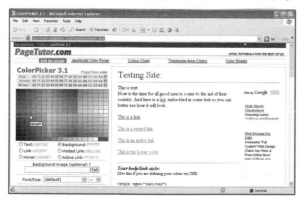

Figure 1-7   The color picker

11

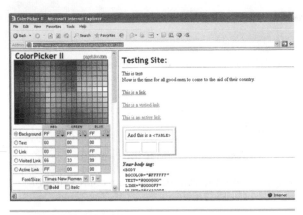

Figure 1-8   The ColorPicker II

triplet will appear. You can also use the ColorPicker II, at http://www.pagetutor.com/colorpicker/picker2/index.html, which appears in Figure 1-8, in which you directly enter hexadecimal values to see the resulting color.

Now, we'll start formatting the page—beginning by centering the text and images in the page.

Centering Text and Images: <center>

You can center text and images and other visual elements with the center element:

```html
<html>
  <head>
    <title>
      Meadow Ridge Townhouses
    </title>
  </head>

  <body bgcolor="#fffff5">
    <center>

         .
         .
         .

    </center>
  </body>
</html>
```

Technically, the center element has been *deprecated* in the latest HTML, version 4.01, which means that those in charge of the W3C are now discouraging its use. Then how should you center text? It turns out that, strictly speaking, format-

Link   If you ever need to look up the attributes of an HTML element, take a look at an online HTML reference—there's a good one at http://www.w3schools.com/tags/default.asp.

ting such as positioning text and images, as well as setting display colors and styles, has been officially removed from HTML. These kinds of formatting are now to be done with Cascading Style Sheets (CSS—see Chapter 3).

However, using the center element is still far more popular than using CSS to center text. For that reason, we'll use the center element here.

It's time to give our sample page a heading, which is "Welcome to Meadow Ridge Townhouses."

Creating Headings: <h1> Through <h6>

HTML has a number of elements you can use to style text, including the h1 to h6 heading elements. These elements style text in a large, bold font for headings—you can see an example, "Welcome to Meadow Ridge Townhouses," an h1 heading, in Figure 1-5. Herc's what it looks like in HTML:

The headings are *block* elements, which means they usually begin on a new line. The other alternative is *inline* elements, such as text, which don't begin a new line.

It's actually fairly easy to set the font and size you want for heading text using CSS, as we'll see in Chapter 3, but the h1 to h6 headings provide a handy set of built-in headings.

```html
<html>
  <head>
    <title>
      Meadow Ridge Townhouses
    </title>
  </head>

  <body bgcolor="#fffff5">
    <center>
      <h1>Welcome to Meadow Ridge Townhouses</h1>
         .

         .

         .

    </center>
  </body>
</html>
```

The h1 heading is the largest, h6 the smallest.

Formatting Text: Underline, Bold, Italic: <u>, <b>, and <i>

HTML also has some built-in text formatting elements, such as u for underline, b for bold, and i for italics. Here's how we make our h1 heading in our sample page underlined and italic:

```
<html>
  <head>
    <title>
      Meadow Ridge Townhouses
    </title>
  </head>

  <body bgcolor="#fffff5">
    <center>
      <h1><i><u>Welcome to Meadow Ridge Townhouses</u></i></h1>

          .
          .
          .

    </center>
  </body>
</html>
```

You can see the results in Figure 1-5. The built-in text formatting elements in HTML are pretty rudimentary, and you'll find much more flexibility using CSS when you get to Chapter 3.

Inserting Plain Text

If you just insert some plain text into the body of a web page, such as "Send us email at", as shown here:

```
<html>
  <head>
    <title>
      Meadow Ridge Townhouses
    </title>
```

```
    </head>
    <body bgcolor="#fffff5">
      <center>
        <h1><i><u>Welcome to Meadow Ridge Townhouses</u></i></h1>
        Send us email at
            .
            .
            .
      </center>
    </body>
</html>
```

it'll appear in your web page, as you see in Figure 1-5—very nice. This text is followed immediately by an e-mail link.

Creating Hyperlinks: <a>

The link in our sample web page is an e-mail link:

```
<html>
  <head>
    <title>
      Meadow Ridge Townhouses
    </title>
  </head>

  <body bgcolor="#fffff5">
    <center>
      <h1><i><u>Welcome to Meadow Ridge Townhouses</u></i></h1>
      Send us email at <a  href =
        "mailto:info@meadowridgetownhouses.com?subject=Rentals">
        info@meadowridgetownhouses.com</a>!
          .
          .
          .
    </center>
  </body>
</html>
```

You create hyperlinks with the a element. The `href` attribute gives the target of the hyperlink (an URL or a mailto: URL). In this case, we're creating an e-mail link—when the users click the link, their default e-mail program comes up with a new, blank e-mail addressed to info@meadowridgetownhouses .com (and with the subject "Rentals").

Creating hyperlinks is an important topic that will enable you to create e-mail links, clickable menus, and image maps. Stay tuned for the goods on links in Chapter 2.

Spacing Text Out Vertically: \

You can use the break element—`br`—to add a line break to space things out vertically:

```
<html>
  <head>
    <title>
      Meadow Ridge Townhouses
    </title>
  </head>

  <body bgcolor="#fffff5">
    <center>
      <h1><i><u>Welcome to Meadow Ridge Townhouses</u></i></h1>
      Send us email at <a  href =
        "mailto:info@meadowridgetownhouses.
com?subject=Rentals">
        info@meadowridgetownhouses.com</a>!
      <br>
      <br>
        .
        .
        .
    </center>
  </body>
</html>
```

Creating Images: <img>

You can display images with the img element:

```
<html>
  <head>
    <title>
      Meadow Ridge Townhouses
    </title>
  </head>

  <body bgcolor="#fffff5">
    <center>
      <h1><i><u>Welcome to Meadow Ridge Townhouses</u></i></h1>
      Send us email at <a   href =
        "mailto:info@meadowridgetownhouses.com?subject=Rentals">
        info@meadowridgetownhouses.com</a>!
      <br>
      <br>
      <img src="triplex.jpg" width="600" height="339"
        border="1" alt="townhouse">

        .
        .
        .

    </center>
  </body>
</html>
```

Here, we're using the most common img element attributes—src, which tells the browser where to find the image; width and height, which tell the browser how big to display the image, in pixels; border, which, if present, draws a border around the image; and alt, which holds the text you want to be displayed in a tool tip (a tiny window of information that appears if the user pauses the mouse cursor over the image).

All these attributes are optional, except for the src attribute, which gives the location of the image (a local filename or an URL). Supplying width and height attributes makes the browser leave space for the image as it's being

17

loaded—otherwise, the elements in the page will jump around as the image is loaded and already-displayed items are moved around to make room for it.

Images are essential to any business web site. They show products, they generate interest, they pull users in. Use images by all means—but don't clutter up your pages with them.

Creating Tables: <table>, <tr>, and <td>

Notice that the bottom two images are displayed inside an HTML table:

```
<html>
  <head>
    <title>
      Meadow Ridge Townhouses
    </title>
  </head>

  <body bgcolor="#fffff5">
    <center>
      <h1><i><u>Welcome to Meadow Ridge Townhouses</u></i></h1>
      Send us email at <a  href =
        "mailto:info@meadowridgetownhouses.com?subject=Rentals">
        info@meadowridgetownhouses.com</a>!
      <br>
      <br>
      <img src="triplex.jpg" width="600" height="339"
        border="1" alt="townhouse">
      <br>
      <br>
      <table border="1" cellspacing="8">
        <tr>
          <td><img src="side.jpg" width="461" height="383"
            alt="side"></td>
          <td><img src ="chairs.jpg" width="476" height="384"
            alt="chairs"></td>
        </tr>
      </table>
```

```
            .
            .
            .
    </center>
  </body>
</html>
```

You create tables with the table element, rows in that table with the `tr` element, and cells in each row with the `td` (table data) element. For example, here's what a tic-tac-toe board might look like as an HTML table:

```
table>
  <tr>
      <td>x</td>
      <td>o</td>
      <td>x</td>
  </tr>
  <tr>
      <td>o</td>
      <td>x</td>
      <td>o</td>
  </tr>
  <tr>
      <td>x</td>
      <td>o</td>
      <td>x</td>
  </tr>
</table>
```

Why does our sample page display those two images, which you can see in Figure 1-6, in a table? That's to make sure they stay side-by-side—if the users had resized their browser window and the two images weren't in a table, the images would slip and slide around until one was on top of the other.

Notice that in the `<table>` tag, we used the `border` and `cellspacing` attributes. Like any HTML element, table has plenty of attributes—here they are:

- **align**   Specifies the horizontal alignment of the table in browser window. Set to LEFT, CENTER, or RIGHT.

- **background**   Specifies the URL of a background image to be used as a background for the table. All cell contents are displayed over this image. Note that if the image is smaller than the table, it is tiled to fit the table. Set to URL.

- **bgccolor**   Sets the background color of the table cells. You can override this attribute at the row and cell level. Set to an RGB triplet color value or a predefined color name.

- **border**   Sets the border width, set to a pixel width. If you set this attribute to 0, no border appears.

- **bordercolor**   Sets the external border color for the entire table. Set to an RGB triplet color value or a predefined color name.

- **bordercolordark**   Sets the color of the lower and right-hand borders of the external border color for the current table. Set to an RGB triplet color value or a predefined color name.

- **bordercolorlight**   Sets the color of the upper and left-hand borders of the external border color for the current table. Set to an RGB triplet color value or a predefined color name. This border, combined with bordercolordark, can create a frame that looks 3-D.

  - **cellpadding**   Sets the spacing between cell walls and cell contents. Set to a pixel size.

  - **cellspacing**   Gives the distance between cells (and therefore the width of the dividers between cells). Set to pixel values.

  - **class**   Is the class of the element (used for rendering).

- **datapagesize**   Sets the number of records displayed in a data-bound repeated table. Set to a positive number.

- **dir**   Gives the direction of directionally neutral text (text that doesn't have an inherent direction in which you should read it). Possible values: LTR: Left-to-right text or table, and RTL: Right-to-left text or table.

- **height**   Gives the height of the whole table, in pixels.

- **id**   Is a unique alphanumeric identifier for the tag, which you can use to refer to it in, for example, a script or CSS.

- **lang**   Is a base language used for the tag.

- **language**   Is a scripting language used for the tag.

- **style**   Is an inline style indicating how to render the element.

- **summary**   Sets accessibility information for nonvisual browsers. Set to a text string providing a summary of the table.

- **title**   Holds additional information (as might be displayed in tool tips) for the element.

- **width**   Sets the width of the table, set to a pixel value or a percentage of the display area (add a percent sign, %, to such values).

By default, HTML tables don't display borders, and that's perfect for formatting—the fact that you're using a table is invisible to the user if no table borders are showing.

Using Horizontal Rules: <hr>

We'll end our sample HTML page, index.html, with the copyright mark you see at the very bottom of Figure 1-6: "© 2008 Meadow Ridge Townhouses." That mark is under a horizontal rule, which you create with the `hr` element:

```
<html>
  <head>
    <title>
       Meadow Ridge Townhouses
    </title>
  </head>

  <body bgcolor="#fffff5">
    <center>
      <h1><i><u>Welcome to Meadow Ridge Townhouses</u></i></h1>
      Send us email at <a  href =
        "mailto:info@meadowridgetownhouses.com?subject=Rentals">
        info@meadowridgetownhouses.com</a>!
      <br>
      <br>
      <img src="triplex.jpg" width="600" height="339"
        border="1" alt="townhouse">
      <br>
      <br>
      <table border="1" cellspacing="8">
        <tr>
          <td><img src="side.jpg" width="461" height="383"
            alt="side"></td>
          <td><img src ="chairs.jpg" width="476" height="384"
            alt="chairs"></td>
        </tr>
      </table>
      <br>
```

COPYRIGHTING YOUR PAGES

When you're creating a business site, it's very important to copyright each page with the copyright symbol. Copyrighting a page merely means inserting a copyright notice—you don't have to register the page anywhere.

A lot of illicit copying occurs on the Internet, because it's so easy. You have no legal recourse unless your pages are copyrighted, so make sure you do copyright them. It takes only a moment and will make potential pirates at least pause.

Trademarks (™) and registered trademarks (®) are a different story; you can trademark terms by marking them with a *TM,* but turning that TM into a registered trademark is a long, drawn-out legal process that can cost a bundle (you've got to show, for example, that no one else used your trademark earlier).

```
        These beautiful townhouses are only four years old, and feature
        a luxurious interior. Each of the townhouses in each of the
        five buildings is large (about 1600 square feet), quiet, has
        three floors, two to three bedrooms, two bathrooms, walk-in
        closet, finished basement, refrigerator, stove, dishwasher,
        and outside deck. The insides are very sharp; lawn maintenance
        and snow plowing are included. They're in a beautiful setting.
        <br>
      </center>
      <hr>
      <center><i>&copy; 2008 Meadow Ridge Townhouses</i></center>
   </body>
</html>
```

You create a copyright symbol, ©, in HTML with the *entity reference,*
©, and the result appears in Figure 1-6.

Uploading Your Web Page

After creating your web page—an HTML document, with the extension
.html—you have to upload it to your Internet service provider (ISP) to go
live on the Internet. Uploading web pages typically demands using FTP (File
Transfer Protocol) client software, and you can see some such programs in
Table 1-2 on following page.

Besides the software listed in Table 1-2, your ISP might have a proprietary
way of uploading HTML documents as well (often involving Upload buttons in
their web pages). If you want a free FTP client, try Internet Explorer—just enter
the FTP address of your ISP (starts with *ftp://*, not *http://*) in the address bar.

Once you're connected to your ISP's FTP server, uploading your web pages
is usually just a matter of dragging and dropping them into the window that
represents your directory in your ISP. If you're having trouble or are unfamil-
iar with the process, give your ISP a call, or take a look at your FTP client's
documentation (assuming any exists).

AbleFtp	AbsoluteTelnet SFTP	AceFTP	ALFTP
AmiTradeCenter	BitKinex FTP	BulletProof FTP	Captain FTP
Classic FTP	CoreFTP	CrossFTP	cURL
CurlFtpFS	CuteFTP	Cyberduck	Directory Opus
eFtp Client	Exceed	F-IT	FAR Manager
Fetch	FileZilla	FireFTP	FlashFXP
Fling FTP	Freely	FTP Commander	FtpCube
FTPEditor	FTP Explorer	FTPRush	FTP Voyager
Fugu	gFTP	Global Downloader	Glub Tech Secure FTP
Interarchy	Kasablanca	KFTPGrabber	lftp
MacFusion	Microsoft Internet Explorer	Mosaic	MOVEit
NcFTP	net2ftp	Red Bird	Robo-FTP
SecureFX	SftpDrive	SFTPPlus	SFX
SmartFTP	Sysax FTP	Transmit	WebDrive
WinSCP	WISE-FTP	WS FTP	

Table 1-2   Some FTP Clients

Validating Your HTML

When creating business sites, it's important that all your web pages say what you want them to say. Any confusion in your HTML might mean your page will be displayed in different ways by different browsers.

For that reason, you should run your pages through an HTML validator before putting them up. If it ever comes down to legal complications over the interpretation of your HTML, you can point out that your HTML is correct and that any misinterpretation is an error.

MEMO

Although validating your HTML is useful, XML validation is more meticulous; the rules are more plentiful and strict. That's why many business sites don't write in HTML—they write in XHTML, the version of HTML written entirely in XML. Many major business sites such as the USA Today site are written in XHTML—but browsers interpret the pages just like HTML. XHTML can be checked much more rigorously for possible errors than straight HTML, and for that reason, you'll see more on XHTML in the next chapter, including how to write and validate it.

There are a number of HTML validators around, but for business sites, I recommend the W3C site (W3C are, after all, the people behind HTML) at http://validator.w3.org/#validate_by_upload+with_options.

Before using the HTML validator, we have to indicate what version of HTML we're writing our document in. The latest version of HTML is 4.01; we'll use that. As I mentioned earlier in connection with the center element, a bunch of elements and attributes (which have to do with formatting and displaying your page) were deprecated in HTML 4.01 by W3C in favor of CSS style sheets, but most of those deprecated elements are still in widespread use. So the W3C lets you indicate if your document is HTML 4.01 Strict (which excludes all the deprecated elements and attributes) or HTML 4.01 Transitional (which allows them). HTML 4.01 Transitional is by far the most popular choice.

You indicate the version of HTML you're targeting with a `<!DOCTYPE>` element, which is borrowed from XML, and which looks like this (it's always placed at the very beginning of a document):

```
<!DOCTYPE html PUBLIC "-//W3C//DTD HTML 4.01 Transitional//EN"
"http://www.w3.org/TR/html4/loose.dtd">
<html>
  <head>
    <title>
      Meadow Ridge Townhouses
    </title>
  </head>

  <body bgcolor="#fffff5">
      .
      .
      .
  </body>
</html>
```

This `<!DOCTYPE>` element points to the Document Type Definition (DTD) for HTML (DTDs are another aspect of XML), which gives the syntax rules for HTML. To validate our sample document, index.html, go to the W3C URL and

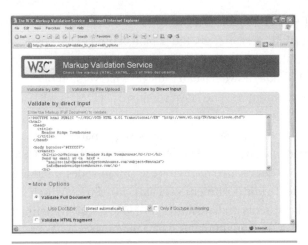

Figure 1-9   Validating an HTML document

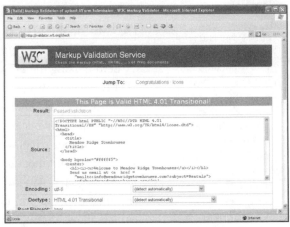

Figure 1-10   A successful document validation

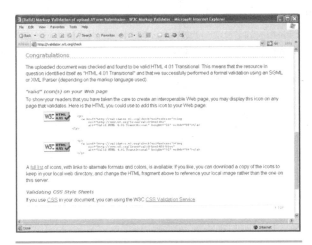

Figure 1-11   Valid HTML 4.01 badges

paste in the document, as you see in Figure 1-9.

Then click the Check button at the bottom of the page (off the screen in Figure 1-9) to validate the document. You can see the result in Figure 1-10—the document validates as HTML 4.01 Transitional. Congratulations!

The actual process isn't as easy as it appears to be here—on a typical business page of any length and complexity, you'll see dozens of errors. The W3C validator does explain the errors, however, giving you a leg up on fixing them—and it's important to get your pages correct to avoid the possibility of customers misinterpreting what the pages say.

Scrolling down in Figure 1-10 brings into view some HTML, shown in Figure 1-11, which you can embed in your page to display the official validation approval badges of the W3C. If you watch for badges like that, you'll sometimes see them on business sites, particularly the XHMTL badges.

HTML Tricks

A business site should create the best impression possible on customers while being easy to use. Every advantage counts, including having a site that is cool and snazzy. This chapter is all about HTML tricks designed to give you an edge. From the basics, such as using frames, to more advanced techniques, such as using Dynamic HTML, you'll find a smorgasbord of powerful HTML effects here: creating image maps, using links to create navigation bars, updating text on the fly, drawing logos, downloading images on the fly, creating visual effects, setting element visibility, XHTML—this chapter is designed to help you boost your web pages from ordinary to extraordinary.

We'll start with a fun one—drawing logos.

Drawing Logos

Cool logos are part of any professional site, but logos can cost a bundle to have designed. Many sites online will help you draw your own logos (and buttons). My favorite such site is www.cooltext.com, which you can see in Figure 2-1.

Cool Text is a fun site that includes, although you can't see it in the figure, animated styles. The Burning style, for example, is made of animated frames. To add text to your logo style, just click that style. We'll use the Carved style here; clicking that style opens the style design page you see in Figure 2-2.

Enter the text you want in your new logo ("Business Sites" in this example) and click the Render Logo button. Cool Text will draw your new logo and display it as you see in Figure 2-3.

To download the image, click the Download Image link you see in Figure 2-3, or right-click the image and select the Save Picture As (Internet Explorer) or Save Image As (Firefox) menu item. By default, your logo is created as a JPG file.

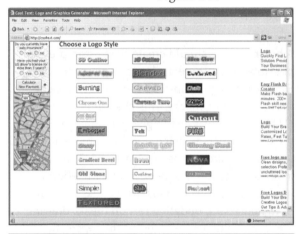

Figure 2-1 Cool Text web site

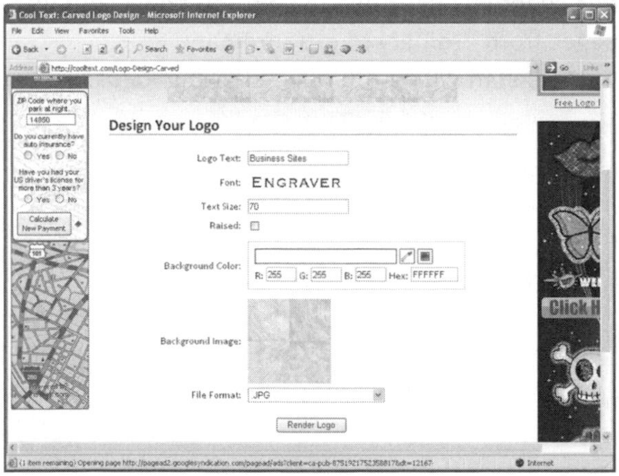

Figure 2-2 The style design page

Changing Text On the Fly

HTML—through the use of Dynamic HTML—allows you to update text and images in your web page. Let's get started with Dynamic HTML by showing how to update text on the fly in a web page.

We'll have three buttons in this example, and use JavaScript to get the Dynamic HTML going. Yes, we're looking ahead here by using JavaScript, but a lot of Dynamic HTML demands it. We start with an innocent web page with the text "Select your option..." in a <div> element, which is used in HTML to mark sections of text:

Figure 2-3   A new logo

```
<html>
  <head>
    <title>
      Updating text
    </title>
  </head>

  <body>
    <h1>Updating text on the fly</h1>
    <div id="div1">Select your option...</div>
  </body>
</html>
```

We'll add three buttons to allow the user to select among Option 1, Option 2, and Option 3 (more on buttons and JavaScript coming up in Chapter 4):

```
<html>
  <head>
    <title>
      Updating text
    </title>
  </head>

  <body>
    <h1>Updating text on the fly</h1>
    <div id="div1">Select your option...</div>
    <form>
```

29

We're using JavaScript here, but if you're not familiar with JavaScript, don't worry—the full details are coming up in Chapter 4.

```
      <center>
        <input type="button" onclick="option1()" value="Option 1">
        <input type="button" onclick="option2()" value="Option 2">
        <input type="button" onclick="option3()" value="Option 3">
      </center>
    </form>
  </body>
</html>
```

Button 1 is connected to the JavaScript function option1, button 2 to option2, and so on, so let's add those functions in a <script> element in the page's <head> section:

```
<html>
  <head>
    <title>
      Updating text
    </title>
    <script  language = "javascript">
      function option1()
      {
          .
          .
          .
      }

      function option2()
      {
          .
          .
          .
      }

      function option3()
      {
          .
          .
          .
      }

    </script>
```

```
      </head>

      <body>
        <h1>Updating text on the fly</h1>
        <div id="div1">Select your option...</div>
        <form>
          <center>
            <input type="button" onclick="option1()" value="Option 1">
            <input type="button" onclick="option2()" value="Option 2">
            <input type="button" onclick="option3()" value="Option 3">
          </center>
        </form>
      </body>
    </html>
```

Here's the Dynamic HTML part. When the user clicks a button, we will replace the text in the <div> element, so we start by getting a JavaScript object corresponding to that <div> element:

```
<html>
  <head>
    <title>
      Updating text
    </title>
    <script  language = "javascript">
      function option1()
      {
        var div1 = document.getElementById("div1");
        .
        .
        .
      }

      function option2()
      {
        var div1 = document.getElementById("div1");
        .
        .
        .
      }

      function option3()
```

```
        {
          var div1 = document.getElementById("div1");
          .
          .
          .
        }

    </script>
  </head>

  <body>
    <h1>Updating text on the fly</h1>
    <div id="div1">Select your option...</div>
    <form>
      <center>
        <input type="button" onclick="option1()" value="Option 1">
        <input type="button" onclick="option2()" value="Option 2">
        <input type="button" onclick="option3()" value="Option 3">
      </center>
    </form>
  </body>
</html>
```

Now you can use the `<div>` object's `innerHTML` property to assign the new text, and that text will automatically appear in the web page. This is the complete, finished example:

```
<html>
  <head>
    <title>
      Updating text
    </title>
    <script  language = "javascript">
      function option1()
      {
        var div1 = document.getElementById("div1");
        div1.innerHTML=

         "Good choice! Option 1 will cost you $2000.00";
      }
```

```
                    function option2()
                    {
                      var div1 = document.getElementById("div1");
                      div1.innerHTML=


                        "Good choice! Option 2 will cost you $3000.00";
                    }

                    function option3()
                    {
                      var div1 = document.getElementById("div1");
                      div1.innerHTML=


                        "Good choice! Option 3 will cost you $4000.00";
                    }

                </script>
              </head>

              <body>
                <h1>Updating text on the fly</h1>
                <div id="div1">Select your option...</div>
                <form>
                  <center>
                    <input type="button" onclick="option1()" value="Option 1">
                    <input type="button" onclick="option2()" value="Option 2">
                    <input type="button" onclick="option3()" value="Option 3">
                  </center>
                </form>
              </body>
            </html>
```

33

That's it. You can see this new web page, text
.html, in Figure 2-4, along with the three buttons.

Figure 2-4   Clicking a button modifies this web page.

A good way to test these example HTML documents is to copy the code from this book's web site, save the code to an HTML file, and then open the file in Internet Explorer. However, when you do this, the yellow security bar might appear at the top of the page with the explanation that Internet Explorer has blocked content ("To protect your security...") because there is JavaScript in the page. In this case, right-click the security bar, select Allow Blocked Content, and click Yes. You'll then see a message box explaining the dangers of allowing script to execute within web pages. Click Yes to close the message box. Now you can execute the script by clicking the buttons. Depending on your security settings, you typically won't see this problem on pages you install on your ISP and download from the Web.

34

Figure 2-5   Updating text in web pages

Clicking one of the buttons causes the web page to update the text in the `<div>` element instantly, as you see in Figure 2-5.

Now you know how to update the text in a web page at the click of a button.

Loading Images On the Fly

Dynamic HTML lets you instantly update more than just text—you can also update images on the fly. Here's an example page, which I saved as image.html, that starts with a `<div>` element:

```
<html>
  <head>
    <title>
      Loading images on the fly
    </title>
  </head>

  <body>
    <h1>Loading images on the fly</h1>
    <div id="div1">Select your option...</div>
  </body>
</html>
```

We'll add three buttons to display three different images when clicked:

```
<html>
  <head>
    <title>
      Loading images on the fly
    </title>
  </head>
```

```
<body>
  <h1>Loading images on the fly</h1>
  <div id="div1">Select your option...</div>
  <form>
    <center>
      <input type="button" onclick="option1()" value="Option 1">
      <input type="button" onclick="option2()" value="Option 2">
      <input type="button" onclick="option3()" value="Option 3">
    </center>
  </form>
</body>
</html>
```

This time when a button is clicked, we'll replace the text in the `<div>` element with HTML for the `<img>` element corresponding to the requested image:

```
<html>
  <head>
    <title>
      Loading images on the fly
    </title>
    <script  language = "javascript">
      function option1()
      {
        var div1 = document.getElementById("div1");
        div1.innerHTML="<img src='image1.jpg'>";
      }

      function option2()
      {
        var div1 = document.getElementById("div1");
        div1.innerHTML="<img src='image2.jpg'>";
      }

      function option3()
      {
        var div1 = document.getElementById("div1");
        div1.innerHTML="<img src='image3.jpg'>";
      }
```

```
        </script>
      </head>

      <body>
        <h1>Loading images on the fly</h1>
        <div id="div1">Select your option...</div>
        <form>
          <center>
            <input type="button" onclick="option1()" value="Option 1">
            <input type="button" onclick="option2()" value="Option 2">
            <input type="button" onclick="option3()" value="Option 3">
          </center>
        </form>
      </body>
    </html>
```

Figure 2-6   Updating an image in web pages

When the new <img> element is written to the web page, the browser will automatically download the new image and display it.

These images must be accessible to the browser. We're just giving the name of the image file in this example's code, so the browser will assume the image is in the same path (directory or subdirectory) as the web page on your ISP. If you're storing the image someplace else, be sure to give the full URL of the image like this:

```
div1.innerHTML="<img src='http://myisp/
myname/image3.jpg'>";
```

If you're testing this code, put three images (named **image1.jpg**, **image2.jpg**, and **image3.jpg**) in the same directory as the HTM file.

You can see this new web page in Figure 2-6.

When the user clicks a button, the corresponding image is downloaded and displayed, as you can see in Figure 2-7.

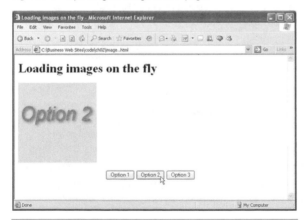

Figure 2-7   A new image in a web page

This is a good technique if you want to display, say, product images. Screen space is always at a premium in web pages, and downloading images as required makes good use of that scarce resource by avoiding crowding too much into your web pages.

Setting Element Visibility

Speaking of preserving screen space and uncluttering business web pages, you can also make items appear and disappear in web pages. For example, you might be explaining about your products and have a button to make a fuller explanation appear. We'll take a look at how that works in a next example, named visibility.html, which starts off with some text in a `<div>` that is invisible, because the `<div>` element's `visibility` style is set to `hidden`:

```
<html>
    <head>
        <title>
            Making elements visible with the visibility property
        </title>
    </head>

    <body>

        <center>
            <h1>
                Making elements visible with the visibility property
            </h1>
        </center>

        <div id="div1" style="visibility:hidden">
            Here's some newly visible text!
        </div>
    </body>
</html>
```

And we'll add a button labeled "Click me" to make the `<div>` element—and therefore its enclosed text—visible:

```
<html>
    <head>
        <title>
            Making elements visible with the visibility property
        </title>
    </head>

    <body>

        <center>
            <h1>
                Making elements visible with the visibility property
            </h1>
        </center>

        <form>
          <input type=button value="Click me" onclick="showmore()">
        </form>
        <p>
        <div id="div1" style="visibility:hidden">
            Here's some newly visible text!
        </div>
    </body>
</html>
```

When the button is clicked, it'll call a function named `showmore` that will
set the `<div>` element's visibility style to `"visible"` like this:

```
<html>
    <head>
        <title>
            Making elements visible with the visibility property
        </title>

        <script language="javascript">
            function showmore()
            {
                var div1 = document.getElementById("div1");
                div1.style.visibility = "visible"
            }
        </script>
```

```
            </head>

        <body>

            <center>
                <h1>
                    Making elements visible with the visibility property
                </h1>
            </center>

            <form>
                <input type=button value="Click me" onclick="showmore()">
            </form>
            <p>
            <div id="div1" style="visibility:hidden">
                Here's some newly visible text!
            </div>
        </body>
    </html>
```

Figure 2-8   visibility.html

Figure 2-9   The hidden text made visible

You can see the results in Figure 2-8, which is visibility.html before the button is clicked.

Figure 2-9 shows visibility.html after the button is clicked—with the new text showing.

Fancy Mouseovers

Ever let your mouse run over some text that changed color as the mouse rolled over it? Here's how that works. (You'll see more on mouse rollovers when we discuss JavaScript in Chapter 4.)

Here's an example, mouseover.html, which turns its text red when the mouse runs over that text. It starts with just the text:

```
<html>
    <head>
        <title>
            Creating mouseovers
        </title>
    </head>

    <body>
        <center>
            <h1>
                Creating mouseovers
            </h1>
            This text turns red when you move the mouse over it!
        </center>
    </body>
</html>
```

Now we'll make that text active—which we do by placing it in a `<span>` element (we could have used a `<div>` element) and setting the `<span>` element's `onmouseover` (active when the mouse enters the element) attribute and `onmouseout` (active when the mouse leaves the element) attribute to a little JavaScript:

```
<html>
    <head>
        <title>
            Creating mouseovers
        </title>
    </head>

    <body>
        <center>
            <h1>
                Creating mouseovers
            </h1>
            <span onmouseover="this.style.color='red'"
                onmouseout="this.style.color='black'">
```

```
                    This text turns red when you move the mouse over it!
            </span>
        </center>
    </body>
</html>
```

Figure 2-10   mouseover.html

The `this` in the JavaScript refers to the current element, which is the `<span>` element, and
`this.style.color` refers to the `<span>` element's `color` style property, which we're setting
to `red` when the cursor moves over it, and `black`
when the cursor moves away.

You can see the result (well, in glorious black
and white) of mouseover.html in Figure 2-10. Although you can't really see it
in the figure, the text is indeed red when the mouse rolls over it.

You can modify other properties of text using this same technique. For example, use the `this.style.fontSize` property to change the size of your
text when the mouse rolls over it.

Handling Links and Menus

Links are a fundamental part of any business web site that's larger than a
single page. You need to give the user some way of navigating from page to
page. The most basic link just appears as underlined text and uses the `<a>`
element with the `href` attribute set to the target of the link:

```
<a href = "page.html">Click me</a>
```

This link appears as the text "Click me" in the page and, when clicked,
makes the browser navigate to the document page.html. Because no full URL
is specified as the target of this link, page.html (the target) must reside in the
same path as the web page document that references it.

You can also make images into links by surrounding an `<img>` element
with an `<a>` element—note we're giving the image no border to avoid having
the browser draw a heavy line around it to indicate that it's a hyperlink:

41

MEMO

The `<span>` element
is usually an inline
element, used when
you want to work with
text that's *inline*—that
is, part of a line. The
`<div>` element is
a multiline element
when text is contained
in its own block
element (that is, gets
its own line in the
browser display).

```
<a border=0 href="page.html">
  <img src="image.jpg" border=0>
</a>
```

Navigation bars are usually made up of a number of link-enabled images arranged in an HTML table to keep them straight no matter how the page is resized. Here's an example—menus.html—that includes both horizontal and vertical menus. Note that we're also using tables to make sure the vertical menus flank the enclosed text in the page, and using the width attribute of the <td> element to make sure the text takes up most of the page. Note also that we're setting the target attribute of the <a> element to "_top", indicating that when the link is clicked, the new page should fill the browser window (the target of all the links is just a sample page named uc.html that reads "Under Construction"):

```
<html>
  <head>
    <title>
      Using menus
    </title>
  </head>

  <body>
    <center>
      <table>
        <tr>
          <td>
            <a border=0 href="uc.html" target="_top">
              <img src="home.jpg" border=0>
            </a>
          </td>
          <td>
            <a border=0 href="uc.html" target="_top">
              <img src="buy.jpg" border=0>
            </a>
          </td>
          <td>
            <a border=0 href="uc.html" target="_top">
```

```
                              <img src="sell.jpg" border=0>
                            </a>
                        </td>
                        <td>
                          <a border=0 href="uc.html" target="_top">
                            <img src="help.jpg" border=0>
                          </a>
                        </td>
                    </tr>
                  </table>
              </center>
              <center><h1>Using menus</h1></center>
              <center>
                <table>
                  <tr>
                      <td>
                        <table>
                        <tr>
                          <a border=0 href="uc.html" target="_top">
                            <img src="home.jpg" border=0>
                          </a>
                        </tr>
                        <tr>
                          <a border=0 href="uc.html" target="_top">
                            <img src="buy.jpg" border=0>
                          </a>
                        </tr>
                        <tr>
                          <a border=0 href="uc.html" target="_top">
                            <img src="sell.jpg" border=0>
                          </a>
                        </tr>
                        <tr>
                          <a border=0 href="uc.html" target="_top">
                            <img src="help.jpg" border=0>
                          </a>
                        </tr>
                      </table>
                    </td>
                    <td width="80%">
```

```
                        Text text text text text text text text text text text
                        text text text text text text text text text text text
                        text text text text text text text text text text text
                        text text text text text text text text text text text
                        text text text text text text text text text text text
                        text text text text text text text text text text text
                        text text text text text text text text text text text
            </td>
            <td>
              <table>
                <tr>
                  <a border=0 href="uc.html" target="_top">
                    <img src="home.jpg" border=0>
                  </a>
                </tr>
                <tr>
                  <a border=0 href="uc.html" target="_top">
                    <img src="buy.jpg" border=0>
                  </a>
                </tr>
                <tr>
                  <a border=0 href="uc.html" target="_top">
                    <img src="sell.jpg" border=0>
                  </a>
                </tr>
                <tr>
                  <a border=0 href="uc.html" target="_top">
                    <img src="help.jpg" border=0>
                  </a>
                </tr>
              </table>
            </td>
          </tr>
        </table>
      </center>
      <center>
        <table>
          <tr>
            <td>
              <a border=0 href="uc.html" target="_top">
                <img src="home.jpg" border=0>
```

```
          </a>
        </td>
        <td>
          <a border=0 href="uc.html" target="_top">
            <img src="buy.jpg" border=0>
          </a>
        </td>
        <td>
          <a border=0 href="uc.html" target="_top">
            <img src="sell.jpg" border=0>
          </a>
        </td>
        <td>
          <a border=0 href="uc.html" target="_top">
            <img src="help.jpg" border=0>
          </a>
        </td>
      </tr>
    </table>
  </center>
</body>
</html>
```

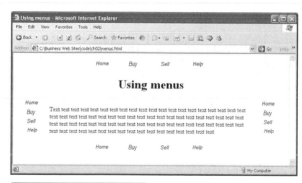

Figure 2-11   menus.html

Whew, that's a lot of nested HTML tables. You can see the results of menus.html in Figure 2-11, where the navigation bars appear at top and bottom, and the two vertical menus at either side. Very cool.

Creating Image Maps

You can also put together image maps using link-enabled images and HTML tables. (We'll see the standard way of creating image maps in the next chapter.) An image map can be a useful way of presenting links to the user in special situations. For example, you could display a map, and allow users to click a particular location within the map—then transfer them to a page where the cuisine of that locale is discussed.

Here's an example, imap.html, which assembles four images, labeled *1*, *2*, *3*, and *4* so you can keep the parts separate, into a single clickable image using a table (note that we're setting the table's `cellspacing` and `cellpadding` attributes to `0` to make the images appear right next to each other):

```html
<html>
  <head>
    <title>
      Using image maps
    </title>
  </head>

  <body>
    <center><h1>Using image maps</h1></center>
    <center>
      <table cellspacing="0" cellpadding="0" border="0">
        <tr>
          <td>
            <a border=0 href="uc.html" target="_top">
              <img src="1.jpg" border=0>
            </a>
          </td>
          <td>
            <a border=0 href="uc.html" target="_top">
              <img src="2.jpg" border=0>
            </a>
          </td>
        </tr>
        <tr>
          <td>
            <a border=0 href="uc.html" target="_top">
              <img src="3.jpg" border=0>
            </a>
          </td>
          <td>
            <a border=0 href="uc.html" target="_top">
              <img src="4.jpg" border=0>
            </a>
          </td>
```

```
        </tr>
      </table>
    </center>
  </body>
</html>
```

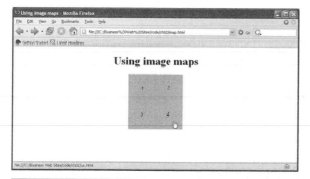

You can see the results in Figure 2-12. While this technique is a quick way of creating image maps, the way tables work differs in different browsers—some browsers will separate the top row of images from the next row with a white line, which spoils the effect of a continuous image.

Figure 2-12　imap.html

Working with Frames

HTML frames are great for making a complex site more compact, because they can display multiple pages in the same browser window. For example, take a look at frames.html, which you see in Figure 2-13.

Clicking a hyperlink in Figure 2-13 opens a new page in the frame on the right, as you see in Figure 2-14. This is a great technique to give customers an overview of your site and to let them click the links to bring up the pages they want.

We start frames.html with a `<frameset>` element, indicating that the left frame takes up 40 percent of the window horizontally, and the frame at right takes up 60 percent of the window horizontally:

Figure 2-13　frames.html

Figure 2-14　Calling up a new window in frames.html

```
<html>

    <head>
        <title>
            targeted frames
        </title>
    </head>

    <frameset cols = "40%, 60%">

        .
        .
        .

    </frameset>

</html>
```

The frame at right will be filled with the hyperlinks you see in Figure 2-13, which are stored in a page named menu.html:

```
<html>

    <head>
        <title>
            targeted frames
        </title>
    </head>

    <frameset cols = "40%, 60%">
        <frame src = menu.html >

        .
        .
        .

    </frameset>

</html>
```

The frame at right is the target of the hyperlinks, so we'll name that frame "display" and start off by displaying a default page in it with the text "Click a hyperlink," as you can see in Figure 2-13. That default page is just named default.html, and we put that into the right-hand frame this way:

```
<html>

    <head>
        <title>
            targeted frames
        </title>
    </head>

    <frameset cols = "40%, 60%">
        <frame src = menu.html >
        <frame src = default.html name = "display">
    </frameset>

</html>
```

Now in menu.html, the page that displays the links at left in Figure 2-13, we'll create those links like this—note that the target attribute is set to "display", the name of the target frame we want to display pages in:

```
<html>
    <ol>
        <li>
            <a href = "page1.html" target = "display">
              Let's see page 1
            </a>
        </li>
        <li>
            <a href = "page2.html" target = "display">
              Let's see page 2
            </a>
        </li>
        <li>
            <a href = "page3.html" target = "display">
              Let's see page 3
            </a>
        </li>
    </ol>
</html>
```

Note that the first page linked to is named page1.html, the second page2

.html, and the third page3.html—we'll create those pages in a moment. First, here's the default page that appears in the left frame, default.html:

```
<html>

    <head>
        <title>
            default [age
        </title>
    </head>

    <body>

        <center>
        <h1>
            Click a hyperlink
        </h1>
        </center>
    </body>

</html>
```

And here's page1.html:

```
<html>

    <head>
        <title>
            page 1
        </title>
    </head>

    <body bgcolor="red">

        <center>
        <h1>
            page 1
        </h1>

            This is page 1!
        </center>
```

```
                    </body>

            </html>
```

And page2.html:

```
<html>

    <head>
        <title>
            page 2
        </title>
    </head>

    <body bgcolor="yellow">

        <center>
        <h1>
            page 2
        </h1>

            This is page 2!
        </center>
    </body>

</html>
```

And page3.html:

```
<html>

    <head>
        <title>
            page 3
        </title>
    </head>

    <body bgcolor="pink">

        <center>
        <h1>
            page 3
```

```
        </h1>

          This is page 3!
        </center>
    </body>

</html>
```

Great—the result of frames.html is as you see it in Figure 2-13, and when you click a link, the linked-to page appears in the right-hand frame.

Opening New Windows

Alternatively, you can spawn new windows—open web pages in separate browser windows. Just assign the `target` attribute the name you want to give to the new window. Here's an example, newwindow.html, which has three links to open three new windows:

```
<html>
    <ol>
        <li>
            <a href = "page1.html" target = "newwindow">
            Let's see page 1
            </a>
        </li>
        <li>
            <a href = "page2.html" target = "newwindow">
            Let's see page 2
            </a>
        </li>
        <li>
            <a href = "page3.html" target = "newwindow">
            Let's see page 3
            </a>
        </li>
    </ol>
</html>
```

You can see newwindow.html in Figure 2-15.

Clicking one of the links in Figure 2-16 opens a new window, as you see in Figure 2-17.

MEMO

You can also create image links that look like tabs, and by using a target `<iframe>`, which is a floating frame you can position in your browser window, you can create tabbed pages, giving the appearance of a folder with tabs that opens to any page your customer wants.

Figure 2-15　newwindow.html

THE EASY WAY

Want to avoid showing the frame border that appears vertically in Figures 2-13 and 2-14? You can remove that border by setting the `<frameset>` border attribute to `"0"` like this:

```
<html>

    <head>
        <title>
            targeted frames
        </title>
    </head>

    <frameset cols = "40%, 60%"
border="0">
        <frame src = menu.html >
        <frame src = default.html name =
"display">
    </frameset>

</html>
```

And the result appears in Figure 2-15—no borders to the frame.

Figure 2-16　frames.html without borders

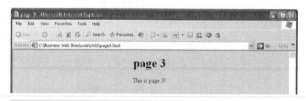

Figure 2-17　Opening a new browser window

Some users, however, are annoyed when a site spawns new windows—filling their desktop with multiple open browser windows. In general, unless you have a compelling reason to produce new windows, it's best to link to pages that replace what's currently in the browser. Most professional business sites, such as eBay, remain self-contained and don't open additional browser windows when the user clicks a link internal to the site.

Using XHTML

As mentioned in Chapter 1, many business web sites, such as usatoday.com, are written in Extensible Hypertext Markup Language (XHTML), not HTML. XHTML is actually XML where the XML elements have the same name as the standard HTML elements, so to browsers, the document looks like HTML.

But an XHTML document can be very rigorously validated for correctness, making sure there are minimal differences from what you intended to display. You can validate XHTML documents with the W3C validator at http://validator.w3.org/#validate_by_input.

We don't have the space here to introduce XML and XHTML, but we'll go through an example. Here's an XHTML document, xhtml.html (XHTML documents have the extension .html or .htm so browsers will treat them like HTML):

```
<?xml version="1.0"?>
<!DOCTYPE html PUBLIC "-//W3C//DTD XHTML 1.0 Transitional//EN"
"http://www.w3.org/TR/xhtml1/DTD/xhtml1-transitional.dtd">
<html xmlns="http://www.w3.org/1999/xhtml" xml:lang="en" lang="en">
    <head>
        <title>
            Welcome to my page
        </title>
    </head>

    <body>
        <h1>
            Welcome to XHTML!
        </h1>
        Here's my page.
        <br>
        Do you like it?
    </body>
</html>
```

Note that this looks just like an HTML document, except for the XML declaration that makes up the first line and the required <!DOCTYPE> element indicating that this document is written to be XHTML 1.0 Transitional (the closest version to HTML 4.01 Transitional).

And adding that element is all it takes for this example to be XHTML rather than HTML. It turns out that the W3C has a number of requirements for documents before they can be called true XHTML documents. Here's the list of requirements documents must meet:

- The document must successfully validate against one of the W3C XHTML Document Type Definitions (DTDs).

- The document element must be `<html>`.

- The document element, `<html>`, must set an XML namespace for the document, using the `xmlns` attribute. This namespace must be `http://www.w3.org/1999/xhtml`.

- There must be a `<!DOCTYPE>` element, and it must appear before the document element.

As an XHTML author, you must bear in mind several differences between HTML and XHTML—again, mostly having to do with the difference between XML and HTML. Here's a list of the major differences:

- XHTML documents must be well-formed (proper) XML documents.

- Element and attribute names must be in lowercase.

- Non-empty elements need end tags; end tags can't be omitted as they can sometimes in HTML.

- Attribute values must always be quoted.

- You cannot use "stand-alone" attributes that are not assigned values. If need be, assign a dummy value to an attribute, like `action = "action"`.

- Empty elements need to be ended with the `/>` characters. In practice, this does not seem to be a problem for the major browsers, which is a lucky thing for XHTML, because it's definitely not standard HTML.

- The `<a>` element cannot contain other `<a>` elements.

- The `<label>` element cannot contain other `<label>` elements.

- The `<form>` element cannot contain other `<form>` elements.

■ You must use the id attribute and not the name attribute, even on elements that have also had a name attribute. In XHTML 1.0, the name attribute of the \<a>, \<applet>, \<form>, \<frame>, \<iframe>, \<img>, and \<map> elements is formally deprecated.

That's XHTML in overview—if you want more details, take a look at a book on XHTML or XML. XHTML provides your business site with web pages that you can verify according to rules more rigorous than classic HTML. This can help avoid ambiguities or misinterpretations on the part of browsers or customers.

Optimizing Cascading Style Sheets

As of HTML 4.0, most of the display abilities of HTML were removed. Shocking, isn't it? According to the W3C, you're now supposed to use Cascading Style Sheets (CSS) to customize all aspects of your web page visuals, from underlining text to positioning items in your pages.

People never wholly accepted the W3C's ruling on this, so HTML 4.0 split into two versions: Strict and Transitional. Transitional HTML 4.0, the more popular these days, still has all the display elements, while Strict doesn't. That's not to say that working with style sheets is useless—far from it. In this chapter, we'll see what Cascading Style Sheets has to offer us, and as you'll see, the W3C went gaga over them for good reasons. You can do thousands of things with CSS that you can't do with straight HTML. Want a heading to be in a particular font and point size? CSS is your ticket. Want to place text or images at a specific location in a page without having to use HTML tables? CSS is your answer.

After you get a working knowledge of HTML, the next step is to master CSS, which is becoming as important as HTML. That's what this chapter is all about.

Part of CSS is about letting your web page change dynamically by using mouseovers, moving elements,

58

applying different styles, and so on. In this chapter, we'll also look at additional ways to bring your pages dynamically to life: web pages that respond to the time of day and that feature amazing transitions such as wipes or slides.

Using Style Sheets

You have three ways to integrate CSS styles into your web pages: using embedded style sheets, using external style sheets, and using inline styles. CSS style sheets are collections of *style rules,* and each rule is targeted at a particular type of element, such as the <body> element, <p> elements, and so on. The actual styles can be given in curly braces and consist of style *property*: *setting* pairs. For example, in our next example, embedded.html, we're specifying that the <body> element is to have a white background and a black foreground color, <p> elements are to display their text in italic, and the link <a> elements are to be red before they're clicked, blue when the link has already been visited, and green when you're clicking the link:

```
<html>
    <head>
        <title>
            This is a web page
        </title>

        <style type="text/css">
            body {background: white; color: black}
            a:link {color: red}
            a:visited {color: blue}
            a:active {color: green}
            p {font-style: italic}
        </style>

    </head>

    <body>
        Welcome to my page.
        <p>
            If you don't like it, you can go to
            <a href="http://www.w3c.org">w3c</a>.
```

```
        </body>
    </html>
```

This example uses an *embedded* style sheet, which means that it has a `<style>` element in the `<head>` section of the document.

Note how this works—the styles are collected into the `<style>` element and apply to the rest of the page. You can see the results in Figure 3-1.

Figure 3-1   Using an embedded style sheet

Now let's look at external style sheets.

Using External Style Sheets

You can also store style rules in an external file, usually given the extension .css. Here's an example that uses the `<link>` HTML element and the `rel` attribute to connect to an external style sheet named style.css in this new example web page called external.html:

```
<html>
    <head>
        <title>
            Using an external style sheet
        </title>

        <link rel="stylesheet" href="style.css">

    </head>

    <body>

        <center>

            <h1>
                Using an external style sheet
            </h1>

            <p>
            This page uses an external style sheet.
```

```
                    </center>

                </body>
            </html>
```

Here's style.css—note that we're setting the background color of the page's `<body>` element and setting the font used in the page to Arial (something you can't do with normal HTML):

```
body {background-color: #ffffcc; font-family: arial}
a:link {color: #0000ff}
a:visited {color: #ffff00}
a:hover {color: #00ff00}
a:active {color: #ff0000}
p {font-style: italic}
```

Figure 3-2   Using an external style sheet

Save this CSS code in a file named **style.css** in the same directory as the web page that links to it, external.html.

You can see external.html at work in Figure 3-2. You can also use inline styles, coming up next.

Link   W3C even has a validator for external CSS style sheets—see it at http://jigsaw.w3.org/css-validator/.

Using Inline Styles

You can assign CSS style rules for an element by using the element's `style` attribute. Here's an example that displays a tic-tac-toe board in various colors, inline.html:

```
                    <html>
                        <head>
                            <title>
                                Using inline styles
                            </title>
                        </head>

                        <body>
                        <center>
```

60

```
<h1>Using inline styles</h1>
<table border="2">
  <tr>
    <th style="background-color: rgb(255, 0, 0)">tic</th>
    <th style="background-color: rgb(255, 0, 0)">tac</th>
    <th style="background-color: rgb(255, 0, 0)">toe</th>
  </tr>
  <tr>
    <td style="background-color: rgb(255, 255, 255)">x</td>
    <td style="background-color: rgb(0, 0, 0); color:
      rgb(255, 255, 255)">
      o
    </td>
    <td style="background-color: rgb(255, 255, 255)">x</td>
  </tr>
  <tr>
    <td style="background-color: rgb(0, 0, 0); color:
      rgb(255, 255, 255)">
      o
    </td>
    <td style="background-color: rgb(255, 255, 255)">x</td>
    <td style="background-color: rgb(0, 0, 0); color:
      rgb(255, 255, 255)">
      o
    </td>
  </tr>
  <tr>
    <td style="background-color: rgb(255, 255, 255)">x</td>
    <td style="background-color: rgb(0, 0, 0); color:
      rgb(255, 255, 255)">
      o
    </td>
    <td style="background-color: rgb(255, 255, 255)">x</td>
  </tr>
</table>
</center>
</body>
</html>
```

61

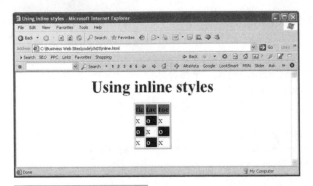

Figure 3-3   Using inline styles

You can see inline.html at work in Figure 3-3. Besides using the style techniques we've seen, you can also define whole style classes.

Using Style Classes

You can define style classes that you can then apply to the elements in your pages.

For example, you might have a class named "red" that defines the foreground (text) color as red (you can also add other styles to the red class, such as selecting a font, and so on). You define the red class as .red in a style sheet to indicate it's a general style class. You can also define style classes that can only be used with certain elements. For example, p.big is a style class named "big" that can only be used with <p> elements. Here's an example, class.html, that shows how to use style classes. Note that after you've defined a class, you can use it with an HTML element's class attribute:

```
<html>
    <head>
        <title>Using style classes</title>
        <style type="text/css">
            body {background: white; color: black}
            a:link {color: red}
            a:visited {color: blue}
            a:active {color: green}
            p.big {font-size: 18pt}
            .red {color: red}
        </style>
    </head>

    <body>
        <center>
            <h1>
                Using style classes
            </h1>
        </center>
```

```
Welcome to my page!
if you don't like it, you can go to
<a href="http://www.w3c.org">w3c</a>.

<p>
Here's some normal paragraph text.

<p class="big">
Here's some bigger paragraph text.

<p>
Here's some <span class="red">text in red</span>.
</body>
</html>
```

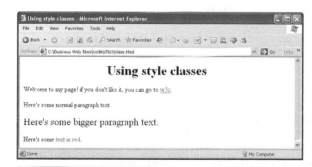

Figure 3-4 Using style classes

You can see class.html at work in Figure 3-4.

Okay, we've gotten an introduction to styles—let's see some more examples showing what else they can do for us.

Styling Text

Working with HTML is okay, but as a business site developer, you probably want more. You want the ability to choose your own fonts and font sizes, for example, to free you from having to use the <h1> to <h6> headers. Ordinary HTML headers are not very flexible because they're pre-formed and only support a few options.

You're in luck—CSS specializes in working with text using style properties like these:

- **font-style**   To make text italic
- **font-weight**   To make text bold
- **font-size**   To set the font size
- **font-family**   To set the font face
- **text-decoration**   To underline the text
- **text-align**   To center the text

Here's what the example using some of these properties, text.html, looks like:

```
<html>
    <head>
        <title>
            Styling text
        </title>

        <style>
            p {font-size: 18pt; font-style: italic; font-family:
                arial, helvetica; text-align: center}
        </style>
    </head>

    <body>
        <center>
            <h1>
                Styling text
            </h1>
        </center>
        <p>
            Here is some text displayed in italics and
            <span style="font-weight: bold">bold</span>,
            as well as
            <span style="text-decoration: underline">
            underlined</span>, in Arial font.
    </body>
</html>
```

Figure 3-5   Using text styles

You can see the results in Figure 3-5.

Here are the style properties you can use with fonts:

- **font-family**   Specifies the actual font, like Arial or Helvetica. If you want to list alternative fonts in case the user's computer is missing your first choice, specify them as a comma-separated list (like this: `{font-family: Arial, Helvetica}`).

- **font-style**   Specifies whether the text is to be rendered using a normal, italic, or oblique face. Oblique is slanted, but the letter shapes are not modified as they are in italic. Used with sans-serif typefaces.

- **font-variant**   Indicates if the text is to be rendered using the normal letters for lowercase characters or using small caps for lowercase characters.

- **font-weight**   Refers to the boldness or lightness of the glyphs used to render the text, relative to other fonts in the same font family.

- **font-stretch**   Indicates the desired amount of horizontal compression or expansion in the letters used to draw the text. Similar to kerning.

- **line-height**   Indicates the height given to each line. A vertical compression or expansion of the text.

- **font-size**   Refers to the size of the font.

And here's an example, font.html, putting some of these font properties to work:

```
<html>
    <head>
        <title>
            Setting font styles
        </title>
        <style type="text/css">
            body {font-style: italic; font-variant: normal;
             font-weight: bold; font-size: 12pt;
             line-height: 10pt; font-family: arial, helvetica;
             text-align: center}
        </style>
    </head>
```

65

```
        <body>
            <h1>Setting font styles</h1>
            <br>
            This text has been styled!
        </body>
    </html>
```

Figure 3-6   Using font styles

You can see font.html in Figure 3-6.

Styling Colors and Backgrounds

Here are the style properties you can use to specify colors and backgrounds:

- **color**   Sets the foreground color

- **background-color**   Sets the background color

- **background-image**   Sets the background image

- **background-repeat**   Specifies if the background image should be tiled

- **background-attachment**   Specifies if the background scrolls with the rest of the document

- **background-position**   Sets the initial position of the background

Here's an example, color.html. In this case, we're styling both the background and foreground of a document:

```
<html>
    <head>
        <title>
            Styling the &lt;div&gt; tag
        </title>
    </head>
```

```
<body style="background-color: #aaffff">

    <div align="left">
        Manager
        <br>
        Slowpoke Products, Inc.
        <br>
        Languid, TX
    </div>

    <p>
        Dear You:
        <div align="center" style="color: red;
           font-style: italic">
            When are you going to ship my order?
        </div>

        <div align="right">
            <p>
            President
            <br>
            NeedItNow, Inc.
            <br>
            Speedy, CO
        </div>

    </body>
</html>
```

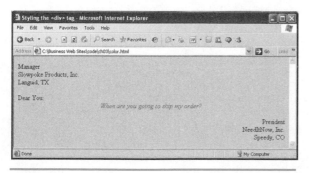

Figure 3-7   Using color styles

You can see color.html in Figure 3-7.

You can also employ CSS to position page elements, and that includes margins and indentations.

Styling Margins, Indentations, and Alignments

Here are the CSS properties you use to work with margins, indentations, and alignments:

- **margin-left**   Sets the left margin

- **margin-right**   Sets the right margin

- **margin-top**   Sets the top margin

- **text-indent**   Sets the indentation of text

- **text-align**   Sets the alignment of text

Here's an example, indent.html, showing how to put some of these properties to work:

```
<html>
    <head>
        <title>
            Setting margins and alignments
        </title>

        <style type="text/css">
            body {margin-left: 10px}
            h1 {text-align: center}
            p {text-indent: 40px}
        </style>

    </head>

    <body>
        <h1>Setting margins and alignments</h1>
        <p>
            This text has been indented!
    </body>
</html>
```

You can see indent.html in Figure 3-8.

MEMO

Now you can see what the cherished `<center>` element is supposed to be replaced with in HTML 4.0—setting the CSS `text-align` style property to `center` like this for `<h1>` elements: `h1 {text-align: center}`.

Although CSS offers you these ways to indent and align text, this is one area where your results will depend heavily on what browser you're using. Make sure you check out the results in Internet Explorer, Firefox, and others—indentations and margins always differ by browser. If you can't get the professional-looking results you want, it's back to HTML tables for positioning.

Figure 3-8 Indenting text

This is one of the major uses of CSS in business web sites—indenting and positioning text without the use of HTML tables.

Changing Your Pages On the Fly

One of the best aspects of CSS is that it lets your web page come alive in a way that straight (static) HTML can't do.

You already know that you can use styles to change text when the mouse passes over it, as in this example I've named bigger.html, where the text grows when the mouse rolls over it:

```html
<html>
    <head>
        <title>
            Using dynamic styles
        </title>
        <style type="text/css">
            body {font-size: 12pt}
        </style>
    </head>

    <body>
        <center>
            <h1>
                Using dynamic styles.
            </h1>
            <span onmouseover="this.style.fontSize = '48'"
                onmouseout="this.style.fontSize = '12'">
                This text gets bigger when you move the mouse over it.
            </span>
        </center>
    </body>
</html>
```

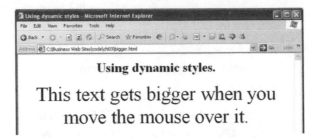

Figure 3-9   Handling mouse rollovers

You can see bigger.html in Figure 3-9.

If you want to do more complex on-the-fly styling, such as changing the font, font style, and color, you can use style classes. This example, changer.html, rapidly assigns style classes to text (note that you have to assign the style class to `this.className`):

```html
<html>
    <head>
        <title>
            Dynamic styles using classes
        </title>
        <style>
            .red {color:red; font-style:italic; font-size:48pt}
            .blue {color:blue; font-size:16pt}
        </style>
    </head>

    <body>
        <center>
            <h1 class="blue" onmouseover="this.className='red'"
                onmouseout="this.className='blue'">
                Move the mouse here to change color and size.
            </h1>
        </center>
    </body>
</html>
```

You can see changer.html in Figure 3-10—here, the font changes to red, large, and italic when the mouse rolls over it.

In fact, handling mouse rollovers over hyperlinks is such a common thing

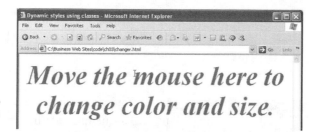

Figure 3-10   Handling mouse rollovers with style classes

to do that there's a special style attribute for hyperlinks— hover —which is assigned the style you want to use when the mouse is over that hyperlink. Here's an example, hover.html, that changes a hyperlink's text to big, red, and bold when the mouse rolls over it:

```
<html>
    <head>
        <title>
            Using the hover attribute
        </title>
        <style>
            a {font-family: verdana; font-weight:
              normal; color: blue}
            a:hover {font-weight: bold; color: red; font-size: 24}
            a:active {font-weight: bold; color: red;
            background-color: darkgray}
            a:visited {font-weight: bold; color: gray;
            background-color: darkgray}
        </style>
    </head>

    <body>
        <center>
            <h1>
                Using the hover attribute
            </h1>
        </center>

            <a href="http://www.starpowder.com">
                Move the mouse over me
            </a>
```

Small Business Web Sites Made Easy

```
                            <a href="http://www.starpowder.com">
                                Now over me!
                            </a>
                    </body>
                </html>
```

You can see hover.html at work in Figure 3-11.

For the ultimate in dynamic, on-the-fly styles, you can toggle whole style sheets on and off. In other words, you can have two style sheets and select which one is active. You do that by setting a style sheet's `disabled` attribute to `true` or `false` to disable or enable the style sheet.

Figure 3-11   Handling mouse rollovers with the `hover` attribute

Here's an example, toggle.html, that toggles between two style sheets at the click of a button through the use of JavaScript (more on JavaScript coming up in the next chapter—this example connects an HTML button to a JavaScript function using the button's `onclick` event, and you'll get all the details on how that works in Chapter 4). Note: This example is for Internet Explorer only.

```
<html>
    <head>
        <style id="dramatic">
            body {font-family: verdana; color: white;
            background-color: black}
        </style>

        <style id="normal" disabled="true">
            body {font-family: 'times new roman'; color: black;
                background-color: white}
        </style>

        <script language="javascript">
            function setstyle(stylename)
            {
                var sheet
                for (var loopindex = 0; loopindex <
                    document.styleSheets.length; loopindex++) {
```

```
                    sheet = document.styleSheets[loopindex]
                    sheet.disabled = true;
                    if (sheet.id == stylename) {
                        sheet.disabled = false;
                    }
                }
            }
        </script>

    </head>

    <body>
        <h1>
            Toggling style sheets
        </h1>

        <center>
            <input type=button value="normal style"
                onclick="setstyle('Normal')">
            <input type=button value="dramatic style"
                onclick="setstyle('Dramatic')">
        </center>

        <p>
            You can set the style sheet for the entire document just
            by clicking a button.

    </body>

</html>
```

You can see the normal style in Figure 3-12 and the dramatic style in Figure 3-13.

Changing web pages dynamically is a very powerful technique. For example, say your business is a restaurant that wants to display a different menu (Breakfast, Lunch, or Dinner) depending on the time of the day.

Here's an example, restaurant.html, that does just that. This example checks the time when the page first loads and creates a menu in an HTML table to match the time using the Dynamic HTML `document.write`

Figure 3-12   Normal style

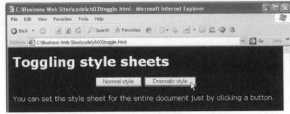

Figure 3-13   Dramatic style

method, which lets you write web pages interactively. (Note also that we're using the `colspan` attribute of table header, `<th>`, elements, which is a cool way of creating cells that span multiple columns in HTML tables.)

```html
<html>
    <head>

        <script language="javascript">
            var datenow = new Date()
            var hournow = datenow.getHours()
            document.write( "<center>")
            document.write( "<h1>")
            document.write( "Welcome to our restaurant")
            document.write( "</h1>")
            document.write( "</center>")

            if (hournow < 5 || hournow > 23){
                document.write( "<center>")
                document.write( "<h1>")
                document.write( "Sorry, we are closed." )
                document.write( "</h1>")
                document.write( "</center>")
            }

            if (hournow > 6 && hournow < 12 ) {
                document.write( "<center>")
                document.write( "<table border>")
                document.write(
                    "<tr><th colspan = 2>Breakfast</th></tr>")
                document.write(
```

```
                    "<tr><td>Pancakes</td><td>$2.00</td></tr>")
        document.write(
            "<tr><td>Eggs</td><td>$2.50</td></tr>")
        document.write(
            "<tr><td>Waffles</td><td>$1.50</td></tr>")
        document.write(
            "<tr><td>Oatmeal</td><td>$1.00</td></tr>")
        document.write( "</table>")
        document.write( "</center>")
        document.write( "</table>")
        document.write( "</center>")
    }

    if ( hournow >= 12 && hournow < 17 ) {
        document.write( "<center>")
        document.write( "<table border>")
        document.write(
            "<tr><th colspan = 2>Lunch</th></tr>")
        document.write(
            "<tr><td>Ham sandwich</td><td>$3.50</td></tr>")
        document.write(
            "<tr><td>Chicken sandwich</td><td>
            $3.50</td></tr>")
        document.write(
            "<tr><td>Cheese sandwich</td><td>
            $3.00</td></tr>")
        document.write(
            "<tr><td>Lobster nuggets</td><td>
            $5.00</td></tr>")
        document.write(
            "<tr><td>Peacock</td><td>$4.50</td></tr>")
        document.write(
            "<tr><td>Chili</td><td>$2.00</td></tr>")
        document.write(
            "<tr><td>Chicken soup</td><td>$1.50</td></tr>")
        document.write( "</table>")
        document.write( "</center>")
    }

    if ( hournow >= 17 && hournow < 22 ) {
        document.write( "<center>")
```

```
                                        document.write( "<table border>")
                                        document.write(
                                            "<tr><th colspan = 2>Dinner</th></tr>")
                                        document.write(
                                            "<tr><td>Lobster</td><td>$7.50</td></tr>")
                                        document.write(
                                            "<tr><td>Filet mignon</td><td>$8.00</td></tr>")
                                        document.write(
                                            "<tr><td>Flank steak</td><td>$7.00</td></tr>")
                                        document.write(
                                            "<tr><td>Tube steak</td><td>$3.50</td></tr>")
                                        document.write(
                                            "<tr><td>Salad</td><td>$2.50</td></tr>")
                                        document.write(
                                            "<tr><td>Potato</td><td>$1.50</td></tr>")
                                        document.write(
                                            "<tr><td>Eggplant</td><td>$1.50</td></tr>")
                                        document.write( "</table>")
                                        document.write( "</center>")
                                    }
                            </script>
                        </head>

                        <body>
                        </body>
                    </html>
```

Figure 3-14   A time-sensitive restaurant menu

You can see the results in Figure 3-14—it's lunch time!

Here's another quick example showing how to update pages on the fly—this time by adding new rows to HTML tables at the click of a button. This example is named newrow.html, and it shows how you can add new items to an HTML table when the page is visible in a browser. This technique is a very handy one—say your page displays the prices of a few products by default, and the customer asks about the price of some other products. Using the

HTML table `insertRow` and `insertCell` methods, you can add additional rows and cells to your table. Here's what the example looks like—it displays a tic-tac-toe board and lets you add new rows at the click of a button:

```html
<html>
    <head>
        <title>
            Creating dynamic tables
        </title>

        <script language="javascript">
            function addrow()
            {
                var newrow = table1.insertRow(3)
                var newcell = newrow.insertCell(0)
                newcell.innerHTML = "x"
                newcell = newrow.insertCell(1)
                newcell.innerHTML = "o"
                newcell = newrow.insertCell(2)
                newcell.innerHTML = "x"
            }
        </script>
    </head>

    <body>
        <center>
            <h1>
                Creating dynamic tables
            </h1>

            <table id="table1" border="2">
                <tr>
                    <th>tic</th>
                    <th>tac</th>
                    <th>toe</th>
                </tr>
                <tr>
                    <td>x</td>
                    <td>o</td>
                    <td>x</td>
```

```
                        </tr>
                        <tr>
                            <td>o</td>
                            <td>x</td>
                            <td>o</td>
                        </tr>
                        <tr>
                            <td>x</td>
                            <td>o</td>
                            <td>x</td>
                        </tr>
                </table>

                <input type="button" value="Add row" onclick="addrow()">

            </center>
        </body>
    </html>
```

You can see `newrow` at work in Figures 3-15 and 3-16.

Want to add more rows? Just keep clicking the Add Row button.

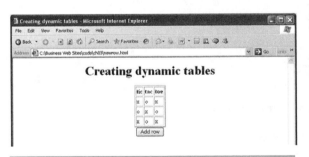

Figure 3-15   newrow.html

Figure 3-16   Adding a new row to an HTML table

Positioning Elements Using Styles

You can use the `position` style property to set the position of elements in a web page. CSS is frequently used for this purpose in business web pages. Here are the properties you usually use when you work with positioning:

- **position**   Can hold values like `absolute` or `relative`
- **top**   Offset of the top of the element's display area
- **bottom**   Offset of the bottom of the element's display area
- **left**   Offset of the left edge of the element's display area
- **right**   Offset of the right edge of the element's display area

Let's see an example that shows how to position elements in absolute terms—the most common way of using the `position` style property. You position elements in absolute terms by assigning the `position` style property the value `absolute` and then actually positioning the element with the `top` and `left` (corresponding to the top left of the element) style properties. Here's how that looks in absolute.html, which positions three colored `<div>` elements. Note that you can position any type of visual HTML element, such as images. If you want to position blocks of text, enclosing that text in `<div>` elements is ideal. In this example we're also setting the height and width of each `<div>` element using the `height` and `width` style properties:

```
<html>

    <head>
        <title>
            Absolute positioning
        </title>
    </head>

    <body>

        <h1 align="center">
```

```
            Absolute positioning
</h1>

<div id="div11" style="position: absolute; top: 80; left: 0;
    height: 30; width: 200; height: 200; background: cyan;
    font-size: 16">
    Hello from CSS!
</div>

<div id="div12" style="position: absolute; top: 120;
    left: 300; height: 30; width: 200; height: 200;
    background: pink; font-size: 16">
    Hello from CSS!
</div>

<div id="div13" style="position: absolute; top: 160;
     left: 600; height: 30; width: 200; height: 200;
     background: yellow; font-size: 16">
    Hello from CSS!
</div>


    </body>

</html>
```

You can see the results in Figure 3-17, where the <div> elements have indeed been positioned as we want them.

In this example, we assigned pixel values to style properties like top and left, but you could also assign percentages (of the browser window) like this:

```
<div id="div11" style="position: absolute; top: 40%;
        left: 10%; height: 30; width: 200; height: 200;
        background: cyan; font-size: 16">
        Hello from CSS!
    </div>
```

You can also use JavaScript to update the position of elements on the fly if you use the JavaScript style properties posLeft and posTop. Here's what some sample code would look like:

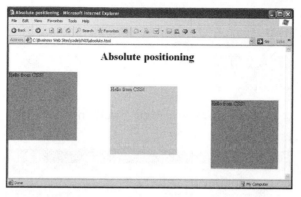

Figure 3-17 Absolute positioning

```
div1 = document.getElementById("div1");
div1.style.posLeft = 900;
div1.style.posTop = 700;
```

Besides absolute positioning, you can also use relative positioning. This technique moves elements relative to where they would normally appear in the browser window. For example, if you use relative positioning, you can position text out of the normal text flow. Here's what that looks like in relative.html, where we're raising and lowering the words "roller" and "coaster" relative to the text's baseline:

```
<html>

    <head>
        <title>
            Relative positioning
        </title>
    </head>

    <body>

        <h1 align="center">
            Relative positioning
        </h1>
        I like
        <span style="position: relative; top: -5">roller</span>
```

```
<span style="position: relative; top: 5">coasters,</span>
do you?

</body>

</html>
```

You can see relative.html at work in Figure 3-18.

Figure 3-18   Using relative positioning

Visual Transitions in Internet Explorer

Let's have some fun. We won't spend much time on the topic, but you can use all kinds of visual transitions when showing or hiding elements in Internet Explorer, and they make for very cool effects. Here are the possible transitions:

- Box In
- Box Out
- Circle In
- Circle Out
- Wipe Up
- Wipe Down
- Wipe Right
- Wipe Left
- Vertical Blinds
- Horizontal Blinds
- Checker Board Across
- Checker Board Down

- Random Dissolve
- Split Vertical In
- Split Vertical Out
- Split Horizontal In
- Split Horizontal Out
- Strips Left Down

- Strips Left Up
- Strips Right Down
- Strips Right Up
- Random Bars Horizontal
- Random Bars Vertical
- Random

Transitions happen when you switch an element's CSS `visibility` property from `hidden` to `visible`. You select a transition with the `transition` property and make it occur with the `play` method. Here's an example, transitions.html, to show how this works. In this case, the user can select which transition to make with a drop-down list box (`select`) control, and click a button with the caption "Start transition" to make the transition happen. To show how elements appear and disappear in transitions, we'll make an image of a flower disappear when a copy of the image is appearing, and vice versa. Here's transitions.html:

```
<html>
    <head>
        <title>
            Using visual transitions
        </title>

        <script language="javascript">
            var transitionduration
            var transitiondirection
            var transitionhappening

            transitiondirection = 0
            transitionduration = 3

            function filterchange()
            {
                transitionhappening = false
```

```
                }

                function handletransition()
                {
                    if (transitionhappening)
                        return

                    div1.filters.item(0).apply()

                    if (transitiondirection == 1){
                        transitiondirection = 2
                        image2.style.visibility = "visible"
                        image1.style.visibility = "hidden"
                    }
                    else {
                        transitiondirection = 1
                        image1.style.visibility = "visible"
                        image2.style.visibility = "hidden"
                    }
                    div1.filters.item(0).transition =
                      select1.selectedIndex
                    div1.filters(0).play(transitionduration)
                    transitionhappening = true
                }

        </script>
    </head>

    <body>
        <center>
            <h1>
                Using visual transitions
            </h1>
        </center>

        <div style="position:absolute;top:270;left:25%">
            <select id="select1">
                <option>box in transition</option>
                <option>box out transition</option>
                <option>circle in transition</option>
                <option>circle out transition</option>
```

```
                    <option>wipe up transition</option>
                    <option>wipe down transition</option>
                    <option>wipe right transition</option>
                    <option>wipe left transition</option>
                    <option>vertical blinds transition</option>
                    <option>horizontal blinds transition</option>
                    <option>checker board across transition</option>
                    <option>checker board down transition</option>
                    <option>random dissolve transition</option>
                    <option>split vertical in transition</option>
                    <option>split vertical out transition</option>
                    <option>split horizontal in transition</option>
                    <option>split horizontal out transition</option>
                    <option>strips left down transition</option>
                    <option>strips left up transition</option>
                    <option>strips right down transition</option>
                    <option>strips right up transition</option>
                    <option>random bars horizontal transition</option>
                    <option>random bars vertical transition</option>
                    <option>random transition</option>
                </select>

                <input type="submit" name="starttrans"
                    value="Start transition"
                    onclick="handletransition()">
            </div>

            <div id="div1" style="position:absolute; width:450;
                height:210; top:60; left:25%;
                filter:revealtrans(duration=1.0, transition=1)"
                    onfilterchange="filterchange()">
                <img id="image1" style=
                    "position:absolute; width:200; height:200;
                    visibility:hidden"
                    src="flowers.jpg" width="256" height="256">
                <img id="image2" style=
                    "position:absolute; width:200; height:200; left:210"
                    src="flowers.jpg" width="256" height="256">
            </div>

        </body>
    </html>
```

You can see some of the transitions that are available in Figures 3-19 to
3-22. It's very cool stuff, and a very dramatic effect, if you want to try it
yourself.

You can use these transitions for entire pages, of course, not just for
images.

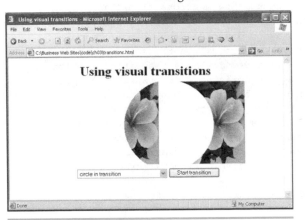

Figure 3-19   The circle in transition

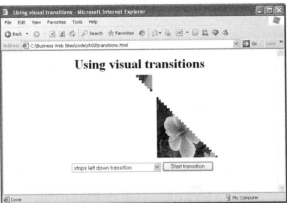

Figure 3-20   The box in transition

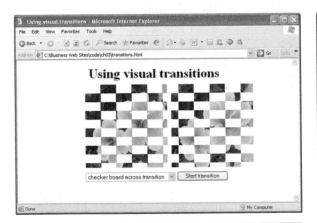

Figure 3-21   The checker board across transition

Figure 3-22   The strips left down transition

Powering Up with JavaScript

Developers of business sites can't afford to ignore JavaScript. JavaScript makes your page come alive in the user's browser (as opposed to server-side scripting with such languages as Java or PHP). The number of things you can do with JavaScript is unlimited—creating snazzy mouseovers, downloading data behind the scenes (using Ajax) without browser refreshes, opening new windows, creating fly-out menus, updating targeted parts of the browser window, using cookies, blanking text fields when they're clicked, making the browser navigate back to its previously opened window (just like the browser Back button), validating data before it's sent to the server—all this and more is possible.

For that reason, in this chapter, we'll look at some of the amazing things JavaScript is capable of. We'll start with a JavaScript tutorial, but please note that there are whole books on JavaScript. Although we'll give you a good working knowledge of JavaScript if you don't already know it, you might also want to check out a good JavaScript book. After the tutorial, we'll dig into just what JavaScript can do for us.

If you're writing JavaScript and coming up with errors, try Firefox—it displays terrific error messages that pinpoint problems in its JavaScript console (accessible from the View menu). Internet Explorer doesn't. Also note that some applications, like Dreamweaver or Microsoft Expression Web, can write JavaScript for you by use of drag-and-drop tools. I find their capabilities very limited, however.

MEMO

If you're storing the samples in this chapter on your disk and using Internet Explorer, you'll run into the yellow security bar a lot ("To protect your security..."). If you see that bar, just right-click it and select Allow Blocked Content; then click Yes.

Digging into JavaScript

JavaScript is usually stored in the `<head>` section of a web page, inside the `<script>` element, like this in the example file I've named javascript.html:

```html
<html>
  <head>
    <title>
      Welcome to JavaScript
    </title>

    <script language="javascript">
      document.write("<h1>Welcome to JavaScript</h1>");
    </script>
  <head>

 <body>
 </body>
</html>
```

If you want JavaScript code executed as soon as the page loads, put the code inside the `<script>` element, but not inside a JavaScript function. If the code is to be executed anytime after the page load, use a function. (Functions will be covered shortly.)

In this example, we're using the `document.write` method (that is, the `write` method of the built-in JavaScript document object) to write to the web page as soon as it loads. Here, we're writing a greeting in an `<h1>` header, as you can see in Figure 4-1.

Okay, that gets us started with a single line of JavaScript. Let's move on and see how to handle data.

Figure 4-1   Executing some JavaScript

Handling Data

You store data in *variables* in JavaScript. Variables are memory placeholders for your data, and you create them with the JavaScript `var` statement. Here's an example, variable.html:

```
<html>
    <head>
        <title>
            Using variables in JavaScript
        </title>

        <script language="javascript">
            var number ;
            number = 366;
            document.writeln("There are " +  number +
                " days in the year 2008.")
        </script>
    </head>

    <body>
        <center>
            <h1>
                Using variables in JavaScript
            </h1>
        </center>
    </body>
</html>
```

89

MEMO

In fact, JavaScript is a very forgiving language—you can omit the `var` statement. The first time you use a variable, JavaScript will automatically create it for you.

Note what's going on here—we created a variable named `number` and then assigned it a value of 366 with the JavaScript assignment operator, =, which stores 366 in `number` here. In JavaScript, operators let you manipulate your data, adding that data or assigning it to other variables. When we used `number` in the third line of the script, JavaScript automatically substituted the value 366 for the word "number". We put the value stored in `number` into a text string by using the JavaScript + operator, and the result here is "There are 366 days in the year 2008.", as you can see in Figure 4-2. Note that this message appears above the header "Using variables in JavaScript"—that's

because the script is executed when the page loads and before the rest of the page loads, which means it writes its text before the browser loads the header. We'll see how to get the message under the header shortly.

Figure 4-2   Executing some
JavaScript

In JavaScript, you can store numbers or text strings or JavaScript objects in variables.

Note that we used the = and + operators in this example, and using JavaScript operators is a very common thing to do with your data. The JavaScript operators are coming up next.

Using JavaScript Operators

JavaScript comes with all kinds of operators to manipulate your data—addition operators, subtraction operators, multiplication operators, and more. Here's an example, addition.html, using the addition operator, +, to add two numbers together:

```html
<html>

    <head>

        <title>
            Using JavaScript operators
        </title>

        <script language="javascript">
            var number ;
            number = 2 + 2;
            document.writeln("2 + 2 = " +  number);
        </script>

    </head>

    <body>
        <center>
            <h1>
```

```
                        Using JavaScript operators
                </h1>
            </center>
        </body>
    </html>
```

Figure 4-3 Using the JavaScript addition operator

You can see the results in Figure 4-3: 2 + 2 = 4.

What operators are available in JavaScript? Here's a list of the most common ones:

- **Addition operator (+)** Sums two numbers or concatenates two strings.

- **Assignment operator (=)** Assigns a value to a variable.

- **Conditional (trinary) operator (?:)** Executes one of two expressions depending on a condition.

- **Decrement operator (–)** Decrements a variable by one.

- **Division operator (/)** Divides one number by another and returns a numeric result.

- **Equality operator (==)** Compares two expressions to determine if they are equal.

- **Greater-than operator (>)** Compares two expressions to determine if one is greater than the other.

- **Greater-than or equal-to operator (>=)** Compares two expressions to determine if one is greater than or equal to the other.

- **Increment operator (++)**   Increments a variable by one.

- **Inequality operator (!=)**   Compares two expressions to determine if they are unequal.

- **Less-than operator (<)**   Compares two expressions to determine if one is less than the other.

- **Less-than or equal-to operator (<=)**   Compares two expressions to determine if one is less than or equal to the other.

- **Logical AND operator (&&)**   Performs a logical conjunction on two expressions.

- **Logical NOT operator (!)**   Performs logical negation on an expression.

- **Logical OR operator (||)**   Performs a logical disjunction on two expressions.

- **Modulus operator (%)**   Divides one number by another and returns the remainder.

- **Multiplication operator (*)**   Multiplies two numbers.

- **New operator**   Creates a new object.

- **Subtraction operator (–)**   Performs subtraction of two expressions.

All right, we've seen variables and we've seen operators. Now it's time to take this to the next level—making decisions in your JavaScript with `if` statements.

Using if Statements

JavaScript `if` statements let your script make choices. For example, are your savings greater than 0 (which is good) or less than 0 (which isn't so good)? You can use the `if` statement to find out. Here's an example, if.html, which checks the value in a variable named `budget` to see if that number is greater than 0. The code checks if `budget` is greater than 0 with the greater-than operator, >, and if the budget is greater than 0, the code displays a reassuring message like this:

```
<script language="javascript">
    var budget;
    budget = -200000.03;
    if (budget > 0) {
        document.write("The value in budget > 0, so the " +
            "budget is still in the black.");
    }
</script>
```

Note what's happening here: the if statement is checking whether the value in its parentheses is true or false; and if it's true, the statement executes the code that follows inside the curly braces.

However, as you can see in the code, the budget is negative, so we don't want to execute the code in the curly braces here. So, how do you execute code if the value in the parentheses in an if statement turns out to be false? You can use an else statement, like this in if.html:

```
<html>
    <head>
        <title>
            Using the JavaScript if statement
        </title>

        <script language="javascript">
            var budget;
            budget = -200000.03;
            if (budget > 0) {
                document.write("The value in budget > 0, so the " +
                    "budget is still in the black.");
            }
            else {
                document.writeln("The value in budget < 0. uh oh!");
            }
        </script>

    </head>
```

```
<body>
    <center>
        <h1>
            Using the JavaScript if statement
        </h1>
    </center>
</body>
</html>
```

Figure 4-4   Using the
JavaScript if statement

94

An `else` statement can (optionally) follow an `if` statement, and if the code in the curly braces in the `if` statement isn't executed, the code in the curly braces in the `else` statement is. You can see the results in Figure 4-4. Uh oh.

Determining Browser Type

Here's a cool way to use the `if` statement—you can check what browser type the user has. That's useful, because different browsers have different capabilities, and you don't want to try something if the browser won't support it. In this example, we check the value in the JavaScript `navigator` object's `appName` property. Properties of JavaScript objects such as the `navigator` object are like variables that are part of that object—they hold data. The `appName` property contains the name of the browser type, which in this case is `"Microsoft Internet Explorer"`. We can check the browser's name with the JavaScript `==` equality operator like this:

```
<html>
    <head>
        <title>
            Checking your browser type
        </title>

        <script language = javascript>
            if (navigator.appName ==
```

MEMO

You can also get the version of the browser with the `navigator. appVersion` property.

```
                    "Microsoft Internet Explorer") {
                    document.write("You have Microsoft


                        Internet Explorer.");
                }


                if(navigator.appName == "Netscape") {
                    document.write("You have the Firefox type.");
                }
        </script>

    </head>

    <body>
        <center>
            <h1>
                Checking your browser type
            </h1>
        </center>
    </body>
</html>
```

Figure 4-5 Getting the browser type

The result in Figure 4-5 appears if you're using Internet Explorer.

Creating for Statements

One thing computers are good at is executing code over and over again, and that's what *loops* are for. Loops let you repeat the same JavaScript statements, performing the same task repeatedly. The most common loop in JavaScript is the `for` loop, and we'll take a look at it here.

Here's an example, for.html, that uses a `for` loop to repeatedly execute the statement `"Hello from JavaScript.<br>"`. This `for` loop is written to execute that statement ten times:

```
<html>
    <head>
        <title>
            Using the for statement
        </title>

        <script language = javascript>
            for(var loopindex = 1; loopindex <= 10; loopindex++){
                document.write("Hello from JavaScript.<br>");
            }
        </script>
    </head>

    <body>
        <center>
            <h1>
                Using the for statement
            </h1>
        </center>
    </body>

</html>
```

Here's how the `for` statement works: the code in the parentheses controls the operation of the loop, and three parts are here, separated by semicolons (;). The first part is the *initialization* part, which is executed before the `for` loop starts executing—here, we set a variable named `loopindex` to 0 in the initialization part. The next part is the *termination* condition, which, when false, terminates the loop—in this case, the termination condition is `loopindex <= 10`. The loop index must be less than or equal to 10 for that condition to be true, so when `loopindex` becomes 11, the condition is false, and the loop ends. The third part is the *end-of-loop* expression, which is executed each time through the loop, at the end of the loop—here, that's `loopindex++`, which uses the JavaScript increment operator (++) to add 1 to `loopindex`. So the `for` loop starts with `loopindex` equal to 0,

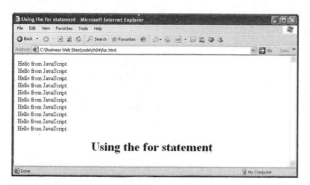

Figure 4-6   Using the `for` loop

`loopindex` is incremented by 1 each time we reach the end of the loop, and when `loopindex` exceeds 10, the loop ends.

Each time through the loop, the statements in the body of the loop—which is the part in the curly braces following the `for` statement—are executed. In this example, that means we'll display the "Hello from JavaScript." message ten times, as you can see in Figure 4-6.

Using JavaScript Arrays

Besides using simple variables, you can also store data in *arrays* in JavaScript. An array is just like a variable that holds multiple data items (named *elements*), and you refer to each item with a numeric index. You can create an `array` named, say, `sandwiches`, with four elements in it with the JavaScript `Array` function like this: `var sandwiches = new array[4]`. Then you can refer to the first data item—that is, element—as `sandwiches[0]` (in JavaScript, an array index always starts at 0), the next as `sandwiches[1]`, and so on, up to `sandwiches[3]`. You can store numbers, strings, or JavaScript objects in each element. The `sandwiches` array is actually itself a JavaScript object, and it has a `length` property that returns the number of elements in it. The `for` loop is a great one to use to loop over—that is, *iterate* over—arrays. Here's an example with four sandwiches, array.html, that displays all four sandwich types using an array and a `for` loop:

```
<html>
    <head>
        <title>
            Using JavaScript arrays
        </title>

        <script language = "javascript">
            var sandwiches = new Array(4);
            sandwiches[0] = "Tuna";
```

```
                              sandwiches[1] = "Turkey";
                              sandwiches[2] = "Swiss Cheese";
                              sandwiches[3] = "Egg and Onion";
                              document.write("Here are the sandwiches:<br>");
                              for(var loopindex = 0; loopindex < sandwiches.length;
                                  loopindex++){
                                  document.write(sandwiches[loopindex] + "<br>");
                              }
                     </script>
                 </head>

                 <body>
                     <center>
                         <h1>
                             Using JavaScript arrays
                         </h1>
                     </center>
                 </body>

             </html>
```

Creating JavaScript Functions

The last topic in our overview of JavaScript is JavaScript functions. A *function* is a section of code that you can execute by *calling* it by name. For example, if you have a function named sum that adds two numbers, you can call that function, executing its code, by calling it by name in your code. You can pass data to a function for it to work on by enclosing a comma-separated list of values in parentheses following the function name. In this next example, the function adds two numbers, so we'll pass the two numbers we want to add to the sum function. Functions can also return data to you; we'll want the sum function to return the sum of the two numbers.

Here's what it looks like in code, function.html. We create the function named sum with the JavaScript function statement and enclose in parentheses following the function name the names of the *arguments* passed to the function:

```
<script language = javascript>
    function sum(value1, value2)
    {
        .
        .
        .
    }
</script>
```

We will add, say, 2 plus 2, with the sum function by calling it this way:
`sum(2, 2)`. In that case, the argument `value1` will contain 2, and so will
the argument `value2`. We can refer to those arguments by name in the function's code. The code goes into the body of the function, which is surrounded
by curly braces. In this case, we want the sum function to return the sum
of the two numbers, and you can make a function return values with the
`return` statement. Here's how we return the sum of `value1` and `value2`:

```
<script language = javascript>
    function sum(value1, value2)
    {
        return(value1 + value2);
    }
</script>
```

Great, that completes the sum function. (Although this function only
contains a single JavaScript statement, there is no limit to the number of
statements you can place in the body of a function.) When we call that function like this: `sum(2, 2)`, JavaScript will pass your data to the function and
replace `sum(2, 2)` with the value returned by the function. Here's what the
whole example, function.html, looks like:

```
<html>
    <head>
        <title>
            Using JavaScript functions
        </title>

        <script language = javascript>
```

```
                        document.write("The sum of 2 + 2 is " +  sum(2, 2));

                        function sum(value1, value2)
                        {
                            return(value1 + value2);
                        }
                    </script>
                </head>

                <body>
                    <center>
                        <h1>
                            Using JavaScript functions
                        </h1>
                    </center>
                </body>
            </html>
```

The result of function.html appears in Figure 4-7. Nice—our data was passed to the function, which processed that data and returned its result.

Figure 4-7 Creating JavaScript functions

Handling Browser Events

So far, our JavaScript has simply executed as soon as the web page is loaded by the browser. However, browsers support many *events,* such as mouse movements or button clicks, that your JavaScript can react to. Here are the common events that JavaScript code reacts to:

- **onBlur**   Occurs when an element loses the input focus (the *focus* is the target of keystrokes).

- **onChange**   Occurs when data in a control like a text field changes.

- **onClick**   Occurs when an element is clicked.

- **onDblClick**   Occurs when an element is double-clicked.

- **onDragDrop**   Occurs when a drag-and-drop operation is undertaken.

- **onFocus**   Occurs when an element gets the focus.

- **onKeyDown**   Occurs when a key goes down.

- **onKeyPress**   Occurs when a key is pressed and the key code is available.

- **onKeyUp**   Occurs when a key goes up.

- **onLoad**   Occurs when the page loads.

- **onMouseDown**   Occurs when a mouse button goes down.

- **onMouseMove**   Occurs when the mouse moves.

- **onMouseOut**   Occurs when the mouse leaves an element.

- **onMouseOver**   Occurs when the mouse moves over an element.

- **onMouseUp**   Occurs when a mouse button goes up.

- **onResize**   Occurs when an element or page is resized.

- **onSelect**   Occurs when a selection takes place.

- **onSubmit**   Occurs when the user clicks a Submit button.

- **onUnload**   Occurs when a page is unloaded.

You can call JavaScript functions when one of these events occurs. For example, say you want to execute a JavaScript function named `clickhandler` when a button is clicked—that is, when its `onclick` event occurs. You could set that up this way when creating the button (which you do with the `<input>` element):

```
<input type="button" value="Click me"
  onclick="clickhandler()">
```

Now you write code for the `clickhandler` function to do something—here's an example, alert.html, where that function displays an alert dialog box with a message:

```html
<html>
    <head>
        <title>
            Handling JavaScript events
        </title>

        <script language= "javascript">
            function clickhandler(e)
            {
                alert("You clicked the button!");
            }
        </script>
    </head>

    <body>
        <center>
            <form>
                <h1>
                    Handling JavaScript events
                </h1>
                <br>
                <h2>
                    Click the button!
                </h2>
                <br>
                <input type="button" value="Click me"
                    onclick="clickhandler()">
            </form>
        </center>
    </body>
</html>
```

The alert box that appears is shown in Figure 4-8—dialog boxes like this one are great for bringing information to the user's attention.

You don't have to display your messages with alert boxes, of course. You can also display your message directly on the web page as text by placing it

Figure 4-8   Showing an alert box

in `<div>` or `span` elements. We've already seen how that works in examples like writer.html:

```
<html>
    <head>
        <title>
            Writing to a page
        </title>

        <script language= "javascript">
            function clickhandler(e)
            {
                var div1 = document.getElementById("div1");
                div1.innerHTML = "You clicked the button!"
            }
        </script>
    </head>

    <body>
        <center>
            <form>
                <h1>
                    Writing to a page
                </h1>
                <br>
                <h2>
                    Click the button!
                </h2>
                <br>
                <div id="div1"></div>
                <br>
                <br>
                <input type="button" value="Click me"
                    onclick="clickhandler()">
            </form>
        </center>
    </body>
</html>
```

You can see the results of writer.html in Figure 4-9, where the text "You clicked the button!" appears when you click the button.

103

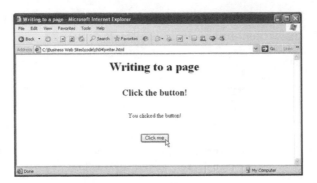

Figure 4-9   Writing to a web page using JavaScript

You can place your text directly into controls like text fields by using the text field's value property like this:

```
var text1 = document.getElementById("text1");
text1.value = "You clicked the button!"
```

That brings us up to speed understanding the basics of JavaScript. In the rest of the chapter, we'll take a look at some cool things JavaScript can do for us, such as opening new browser windows, creating prompt boxes, making the browser return to previous pages, and so on. Note that this is fine as long as things don't get too complex—if you find yourself spending hours on JavaScript, take a look at some prebuilt JavaScript libraries. A good one is the Dojo Toolkit, www.dojotoolkit.com/, which includes all kinds of specialty items like drop-down list boxes.

Creating Prompt Boxes

One way of getting input from the user is to use prompt boxes, which are simple dialog boxes. (You can also read input from HTML controls like text fields, of course, and we'll see that in depth in Chapter 9—there's a preview in the topic after next.) You use the window.prompt method to display a prompt box, passing it the prompt you want displayed and the default text. The method returns the text the user types. Here's an example, prompt.html:

```
<html>
    <head>
```

```
<title>
    Creating a prompt dialog box
</title>

<script language = javascript>
  var text = window.prompt("Enter the text you want to see",
        "Hi there!")

    if (text == "") {
        window.alert("You didn't enter anything.")
    }
    else {
     document.writeln("<center><h1>" + text +
        "</h1></center>")
    }
 </script>
</head>

<body>
</body>

</html>
```

You can see the prompt box in Figure 4-10, with the default text, "Hi there!", showing. Users can enter their own text or just click OK to accept the default text, which is then displayed as shown in Figure 4-11. Note that prompt boxes work, but they're none-too-professional looking. If you want to use a lot of dialog boxes, it's best to create them yourself from new browser windows; that topic is coming up.

Figure 4-10   A prompt box

Figure 4-11   Reading text from a prompt box

Opening New Windows

JavaScript allows you to open a new window using the `window.open` method if you just pass it the name of a new HTML document to open (assuming the new HTML document is in the same directory as the original page) or its location is specified in an URL. Here's an example, window.html (note that you can also pass other arguments to `window.open` to size the new window and make it of various types):

```html
<html>
    <head>
        <title>
            Opening a new window with JavaScript
        </title>
        <script language = "javascript">
            function showglossary()
            {
                window.open("glossary.html")
            }
        </script>
    </head>

    <body>
        <form>
            <center>
                <br>
                <h1>
                    Opening a new window with JavaScript
                </h1>
                <br>
                <br>
                <input type = button value = "See glossary"
                onclick = "showglossary()">
```

```
                                    </center>
                                </form>

                            </body>

                        </html>
```

Figure 4-12   window.html

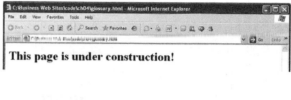

Figure 4-13   A new window

You can see window.html in Figure 4-12. When you click the button, the example opens a new window, glossary.html (which is "under construction"), as you can see in Figure 4-13.

Reading Text from Text Fields and Navigating to New Pages

You can read text the user has entered into a text field by using the `text` field's `value` property. Here's an example, goto.html, that lets the user navigate to a new page by typing its URL into a text field and clicking a button. (Note: you have to enter full URLs, including `http://`, such as `http://www.usatoday.com`.) The script gets an object corresponding to the text field and assigns the value (that is, the text in the text field) to the `window.location` property to make the browser navigate to that URL:

```
<html>
    <head>
        <title>
            Navigating to a new URL using JavaScript
```

```
                         </title>

                         <script language = "javascript">
                             function goto()
                             {
                                 var text1 = document.getElementById("text1");
                                 window.location = text1.value;
                             }
                         </script>

                  </head>

                  <body>
                      <center>
                          <h1>
                              Navigating to a new URL using JavaScript
                          </h1>

                          <form>
                              <br>
                              <input type = text id = "text1" size = "60">
                              <br>
                              <br>
                              <input type = button value = "navigate"
                                onclick = "goto()">
                          </form>

                      </center>

                  </body>

          </html>
```

And that's how you read text from text fields—by using the `text` field's
`value` property.

Navigating with History

For that matter, you can also mimic the browser's Forward and Back buttons
with the `history` object, which is accessible with the `history` property of

the `window` object. You can use the `back` method of the `history` object to go back one page, the `forward` method to go forward one page, and the `go` method to go forward or backward as many pages as you like; `go(2)` goes forward two pages, `go(-2)` goes backwards two pages, and so on. Here's an example, navigate.html, that puts the `history` object to work along with a few buttons:

```html
<html>
    <head>
        <title>
            Using the history object
        </title>

            <script language = javascript>
                function goback()
                {
                    window.history.back();
                }
                function goforward()
                {
                    window.history.forward();
                }
                function gobacktwo()
                {
                    window.history.go(-2);
                }
                function goforwardtwo()
                {
                    window.history.go(2);
                }
        </script>
    </head>

    <body>
        <center>
            <h1>
                Using the history object
            </h1>

            <form>
```

```
                                    <br>
                                    Navigate using the history object
                                    <br>
                                    <br>
                                    <input type = button value = "< Back one page"
                                        onclick = "goback()">
                                    <input type = button value = "Forward one page >"
                                        onclick = "goforward()">
                                    <br>
                                    <br>
                                    <input type = button value = "<< Back two pages"
                                        onclick = "gobacktwo()">
                                    <input type = button value = "Forward two pages >>"
                                        onclick = "goforwardtwo()">
                            </form>
                    </center>
            </body>

    </html>
```

JavaScript URLs and Image Maps

Besides calling JavaScript functions when the user clicks a button, you
can also have the browser call a JavaScript function when the user clicks a
hyperlink. Such links are called *JavaScript URLs,* and here's an example
that calls a `javascript` function named `getinfo` when clicked:
`<a href="javascript:getinfo()">Click here</a>`. You can
also use JavaScript URLs in image maps. Such maps are created with the
`<map>` element, with enclosed `<area>` elements. Each `<area>` element has
an `href` attribute that points to the URL to be called when the corresponding
area in the image map is clicked.

Here's an example, imap.html, with a working image map—note that
`link4`, the guestbook link, points to a `javascript` function that displays
an alert box saying the guestbook isn't working:

```
<html>
    <head>
```

```
            <title>
                Using an image map
            </title>

            <script language="javascript">
                function sorry()
                {
                    alert("Sorry, the guestbook is not working.");
                }
            </script>
        </head>

        <body bgcolor="black">
            <center>
                <img width=528 height=137 src="mainmenu.jpg"
                    border=0 alt="image map" usemap="#imap">
                <map name="imap">
                    <area name="link1" shape=rect coords="16,39 127,61"
                        href="http://www.reuters.com" alt="News">
                    <area name="link2" shape=rect coords="62,71 173,93"
                        href="http://www.google.com"
                        alt="Web Search">
                    <area name="link3" shape=rect coords="98,104 209,126"
                        href="http://forecast.weather.gov" alt="Weather">
                    <area name="link4" shape=rect coords="411,35 522,57"
                        href="javascript:sorry()"
                        alt="Guestbook">
                    <area name="link5" shape=rect coords="360,67 471,89"
                        href="http://www.w3schools.com/HTML/"
                        alt="HTML Design">
                    <area name="link6" shape=rect coords="328,98 439,120"
                        href="http://www.web100.com/"
                        "Hottest 100 Sites">
                    <area name="default" shape=default
                        href="http://www.useatoday.com"
                        alt="Image map">
                </map>
            </center>
        </body>
    </html>
```

111

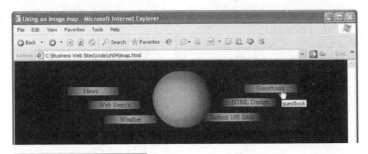

You can see the image map in Figure 4-14. When you click the Guestbook link, the browser pops a JavaScript alert box on the screen, as you can see in Figure 4-15.

If you're using the downloadable code for this book, make sure you place mainmenu.jpg in the same directory as imap.html so your browser can access that image file.

Figure 4-14   An image map

Figure 4-15   Using a JavaScript URL in an image map

Creating Cookies

JavaScript lets you store information in cookies, those snippets of text that store data on the user's machine and then read it later. Here's an example, cookie.html, that sets a cookie that lasts one day and lets you read that cookie as well. We set the cookie, which we'll name greatCookie in a function named setCookie, called when the user clicks a button. There we set the date the cookie expires to the current time plus one day's worth of milliseconds (a millisecond is 1/1000th of a second). Then we store the cookie by assigning its text and expiration time to document.cookie, and flash an alert box on the screen saying the cookie has been created:

```
function setCookie()
{
    var cookieDate = new Date();
    cookieDate.setTime(cookieDate.getTime() +
      24 * 60 * 60 * 1000);

    document.cookie =
        "greatCookie=This is the cookie text.;expires="
        + cookieDate.toGMTString();

    window.alert("Cookie created!");
}
```

When the user clicks another button to read the cookie (either before or after a page refresh—or after coming back to the page at a later time, because the cookie will last for a day), another function is called, `getCookie`. In that function, we use the string search `javascript` function `indexOf` (which returns the character number in a `string` at which the text you're searching for starts) to search for the `greatCookie` cookie. When we've retrieved it, we extract the actual cookie text using the JavaScript substring method, which extracts substrings from text strings:

```html
<html>
    <head>
        <title>
            Working with Cookies
        </title>

        <script language="JavaScript">
            function setCookie()
            {
                var cookieDate = new Date();
                cookieDate.setTime(cookieDate.getTime() +
                  24 * 60 * 60 * 1000);

                document.cookie =
                    "greatCookie=This is the cookie text.;expires="
                    + cookieDate.toGMTString();

                window.alert("Cookie created!");
            }
            function getCookie()
            {
                var cookieData = new String(document.cookie);
                var cookieHeader = "greatCookie=";
                var text1 = document.getElementById("text1");

                var cookieStart = cookieData.indexOf(cookieHeader);

                if (cookieStart != -1){
                    text1.value =
                        cookieData.substring(cookieStart
                        + cookieHeader.length);
```

```
                            }
                            else{
                                text1.value = "Did not find the cookie.";
                            }
                        }
                </script>
            </head>

            <body>
                <center>
                    <h1>
                        Working with Cookies in JavaScript
                    </h1>
                </center>

                <form>
                    <center>
                        <input type="text" id="text1" size="30">
                        <br>
                        <br>
                        <input type = "button" value = "Create the cookie"
                            onclick = "setCookie()">
                        <br>
                        <br>
                        <input type = "button" value = "Retrieve the cookie"
                            onclick = "getCookie()">
                    </center>
                </form>
            </body>
        </html>
```

Figure 4-16 Setting a cookie

You can open cookie.html in a browser and click the Create The Cookie button, which displays the alert box you see in Figure 4-16, confirming that the cookie was set. When you come back to the page, you can click the Retrieve The Cookie button to read the cookie's text, which is displayed in the page's text field, as you see in Figure 4-17. Now that's cool. You can save all kinds of information about your customers this way—their preferences, pending order invoice number, and so on.

Figure 4-17 Getting a cookie

Avoiding Screen Refreshes with Ajax

"Ajax" stands for "Asynchronous JavaScript and XML," and you can use it to access a server (where your web page resides) without having to refresh the user's browser. That is, the browser screen doesn't flash or flicker at all—your JavaScript code accesses the server behind the scenes and downloads data.

A full treatment of Ajax is beyond the scope of this book—many books on Ajax are available. However, we can see an example that uses Ajax to download the text in a file named data.txt from the server behind the scenes and then displays that text—all without the browser navigating to a new page or flickering. This is good for business sites because you don't need to make your customers navigate from page to page—you can download the data behind the scenes and just update the parts of the page that need to be updated. For example, instead of making checkout a five-step process with five different pages, you can check out the user in a single page with no screen flashes (which makes your web application look just like a desktop application).

Ajax uses the XMLHttpRequest object built into modern browsers to contact the server behind the scenes. You configure that object with the URL you want to access, which will just be "data.txt" here, since we'll put data.txt in the same directory on the server as ajax.html. (Note that you can't access servers other than the one your Ajax page came from without doing additional work to get past the browser's security system.) This example just downloads the static text in data.txt, but you can also interact with server-side programs such as those written in PHP, and send data from the browser to those programs by using Ajax.

When you request data from the server, you connect a callback function to the XMLHttpRequest object's onreadystatechange property and use the object's readystate and status properties to monitor the download. When the download is complete, you can recover the downloaded text data from the `XMLHttpRequest` object's `responseText` property. If you're downloading XML, you recover the downloaded XML from the object's `responseXML` property instead. This example will display the downloaded text in a `<div>` element.

In overview, it works like this: the code creates an `XMLHttpRequest` object (the creation process is different in the Internet Explorer and the Firefox browsers), configures the `XMLHttpRequest` object with the URL it's meant to fetch and the HTTP method is to use (we use the `HTTP GET` method here), and then connects the `callback` function to the `XMLHttpRequest` object's `onreadystatechange` property. Then to make the object connect to the server, we call its `send` method. When the server responds, we monitor the download in the `callback` function. When the download is complete and okay, we display the recovered text in a `<div>` element in the page.

Whew. Here's what ajax.html looks like:

```html
<html>
  <head>
    <title>An Ajax example</title>

    <script language = "javascript">
      var XMLHttpRequestObject = false;

      if (window.XMLHttpRequest) {
        XMLHttpRequestObject = new XMLHttpRequest();
      } else if (window.ActiveXObject) {
        XMLHttpRequestObject = new
          ActiveXObject("Microsoft.XMLHTTP");
      }

      function getData(dataSource, divID)
      {
        if(XMLHttpRequestObject) {
          var obj = document.getElementById(divID);
          XMLHttpRequestObject.open("GET", dataSource);
```

```
                    XMLHttpRequestObject.onreadystatechange = function()
                    {
                      if (XMLHttpRequestObject.readyState == 4 &&
                        XMLHttpRequestObject.status == 200) {
                          obj.innerHTML = XMLHttpRequestObject.responseText;
                      }
                    }

                    XMLHttpRequestObject.send(null);
                  }
                }
            </script>
        </head>

        <body>

          <H1>An Ajax example</H1>

          <form>
            <input type = "button" value = "Fetch the message"
              onclick = "getData('data.txt', 'targetDiv')">
          </form>

          <div id="targetDiv">
            <p>The fetched message will appear here.</p>
          </div>

        </body>
    </html>
```

Note: Unlike with the other examples in this chapter, you can't run this one by opening it directly from disk in your browser. The XMLHttpRequest object needs to interact with a web server, so you have to place ajax.html and data.txt on a web server, and then access ajax.html by URL in your browser.

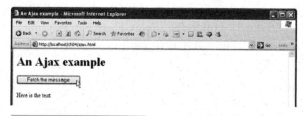

Figure 4-18   Using Ajax to download text behind the scenes

You can see the results in Figure 4-18 (I have the Microsoft Internet Information web server on my computer, which is why the URL in the browser's

MEMO

If you look around the Internet, you'll see more and more sites use Ajax (it was originally considered the foundation of Web 2.0)—take a look at Google Suggest, which uses Ajax to download search term suggestions at www.google.com/webhp?complete=1&hl=en, or Tom Riddle's Diary at http://pandorabots.com/pandora/talk?botid=c96f911b3e35f9e1, which responds to your typed questions without a browser refresh, or www.plasticshore.com/projects/chat/, which is an Ajax-enabled chat program, or a cool mosaic with draggable and droppable tiles at www.thebroth.com/mosaic.

address bar reads "http://localhost"). When the user clicks the button, the example connects to the server behind the scenes, downloads data.txt, and displays the text in that file in the page. No fuss, no muss, no page refresh—it looks like the text just appeared in the page. That's a cool way of giving your web applications the feel of desktop applications, and making life easier for your customers. If you're interested in this, check out a good book on Ajax.

Using JavaScript Validation

Many business pages use JavaScript for user input validation—that is, checking what the user types before sending it on to the server. You know, those pain-in-the-neck dialog boxes you saw that day you didn't enter your phone number in the required format, or neglected to enter your great aunt's birthday.

Here's the way it works. To catch the data an HTML form is attempting to send to the server when the Submit button is clicked, you can assign the name of a JavaScript function to the form's `onsubmit` event. In the function, you check the data the user entered (keep in mind that we'll just check the text in text fields here and will cover other HTML controls in Chapter 9). If that data's not okay, you return `false` from the function. If it's okay, you call the form's `submit` function to send the data on to the server. Here's an example that checks to make sure the user has entered data in a required field:

```
<script language="javascript">
    function checker()
    {
        var text1 = document.getElementById("text1");
        var form1 = document.getElementById("form1");
        if (text1.value == "") {
```

```
                    alert("Please enter some text.");
                    return false
                } else {
                    form1.submit();
                }
            }
        </script>
        .
        .
        .
        <form id="form1" action="www.somepage.php" method="post"
            onsubmit="return checker()">
            Please enter some text:
            <input type="text" id="text1">
            <input type="Submit" value="submit">
        </form>
```

Here's a full example, validation.html, where we'll check if a date the user is submitting is either in the format 12/31/05 or 12/31/2005—and if it's in neither, we'll display an error, stopping the form from being submitted until it's fixed. To check the data, we'll write a JavaScript function named checker; when the form is submitted, we'll have JavaScript call that function. This example is a little advanced in that it uses JavaScript *regular expressions,* which is a way of matching text to check the text's format.

We'll create two regular expressions here, corresponding to the formats *mm/dd/yy* (/^(\d{1,2})\/(\d{1,2})\/(\d{2})$/) and *mm/dd/yyyy* (/^(\d{1,2})\/(\d{1,2})\/(\d{4})$/), and check the date the user has entered to make sure it's in the right format. Here's what validation.html looks like (note that the actual URL this page submits its data to doesn't exist— so just test this example with erroneous data to check if it catches errors):

```
<html>
    <head>
```

119

> **Link** To read all there is to read about regular expressions, check out http://perldoc.perl.org/perlre.html.

```
<title>Verifying user data</title>
    <script language="javascript">
        function checker()
        {
            var text1 = document.getElementById("text1");
            var form1 = document.getElementById("form1");
            var regexp1 = /^(\d{1,2})\/(\d{1,2})\/(\d{2})$/;
            var regexp2 = /^(\d{1,2})\/(\d{1,2})\/(\d{4})$/;
            var result1 =
              text1.value.match(regexp1);
            var result2 =
              text1.value.match(regexp2);
            if (result1 == null && result2 == null) {
                alert("Sorry, that's not a valid date.");
                text1.value = "";
                return false
            } else {
                form1.submit();
            }
        }
    </script>
</head>

<body>
    <h1>Verifying user data</h1>
    <form id="form1" action="www.somepage.php" method="post"
        onsubmit="return checker()">
        Please enter a date:
        <input type="text" id="text1">
        <input type="Submit" value="submit">
    </form>
</body>
<html>
```

Figure 4-19   validation.html

You can see validation.html in Figure 4-19. What I'm entering in the text field is not a date, so we're expecting an error. And sure enough, the error is noticed and displayed in Figure 4-20.

Figure 4-20   Catching a
validation error

Creating Drop-down Menus

We'll close out this chapter with an example showing how to create drop-
down menus. This kind of thing usually takes an immense amount of
JavaScript, so it's usually better leaving it to the JavaScript libraries that you
can use, like Fojo. But there are a bunch of details worth knowing here.

For example, up to this point, we've mostly used the `onclick` event. This
example also uses the `onfocus` event, which occurs when an element gets
the focus (the element that has the focus in a web page is the element that is
the target of keystrokes—indicated, for example, by the blinking text-insertion
cursor, or by a button that is a different color than other buttons on the form);
the `onblur` event, which occurs when an element loses the focus; and the
`onkeyup` event. We'll use the `onkeyup` event to display our drop-down
menu when someone types anything in a text field—the `onkeyup` event
corresponds to a key being released (going up).

Two text fields will be in this example—when you type anything into the
bottom text field, the drop-down menu will appear. The top text field is there
to show another JavaScript technique—when you click it, it blanks any text
in it; you've seen those text fields with prompting text in them ("Enter your
address here.") that blank when you click them.

Also, this example shows how to drop a drop-down menu, which is made
up of a `stled` `<div>` element on top of other elements without causing
those other elements to move around—you have to position the `<div>`
element using CSS absolute positioning. And to avoid having any content
beneath the menu bleed through, we give the menu an opaque white background.

There's one more technique here worth noting. This example may be
shown on computers with all kinds of different screen resolutions, so positioning the menu in absolute terms at the bottom of the second text field
could be tricky, because the position of the text field will be different in different screen resolutions. Can you determine where the bottom of the text field
is by using its bottom CSS property? (In JavaScript, that's the `posBottom`

MEMO

Want to give a control
like a text field the
focus? Just call its
`setFocus` method
like this: `text1.`
`setFocus()`.

property, like this: `text2.style.posBottom`.) No, because the `posBottom` property holds nothing unless you've positioned the text field in absolute terms, which we haven't done for the text field. So you can use the `offsetTop` property of the JavaScript object corresponding to the text field, adding to it the value of the `offsetHeight` property (there is no `offsetBottom` property). Then we position the top of the `<div>` element to the bottom of the text field—no matter how the browser window is resized or the screen resolution varies—like this:

```
targetDiv.style.posTop = text2.offsetTop + text2.offsetHeight;
Here's what the whole example, dropdown.html, looks like:
<html>
  <head>

    <title>Drop-down menus</title>

    <style>
    #targetDiv
    {
      color: #00ff00;
      width: 40%;
      position: absolute;
      top: 135px;
      left: 10px;
      background:none;
    }
    a {text-decoration : none}
    </style>
    <script language = "javascript">

    function handler(e)
    {
      var arrayTerm = new Array(4);
      arrayTerm[0] = "Item 1";
      arrayTerm[1] = "Item 2";
      arrayTerm[2] = "Item 3";
      arrayTerm[3] = "Item 4";
      var arrayTarget = new Array(4);
      arrayTarget[0] = "javascript:f1()";
```

```
          arrayTarget[1] = "javascript:f2()";
          arrayTarget[2] = "javascript:f3()";
          arrayTarget[3] = "javascript:f4()";
          var data = "<table>";

          for (var loopIndex = 0; loopIndex < arrayTerm.length;
            loopIndex++)
          {
            data += "<tr><td>" +
            "<a href='" + arrayTarget[loopIndex] + "'>" +
             arrayTerm[loopIndex] + "</td></tr>";
          }

          data += "</table>";

          var targetDiv = document.getElementById("targetDiv");
          targetDiv.style.border = "1px solid black";
          targetDiv.style.background = "white";
          targetDiv.innerHTML = data;

          var text2 = document.getElementById("textField");
          targetDiv.style.posTop = text2.offsetTop +

            text2.offsetHeight;

        }
        function closer(e)
        {
          var targetDiv = document.getElementById("targetDiv");

          targetDiv.style.border = "";
          targetDiv.style.background = "none";
          targetDiv.innerHTML = "";
        }
        function f1(e)
        {
          alert("You selected item 1.");
          closer();
        }
        function f2(e)
```

```
        {
          alert("You selected item 2.");
          closer();
        }
        function f3(e)
        {
          alert("You selected item 3.");
          closer();
        }
        function f4(e)
        {
          alert("You selected item 4.");
          closer();
        }
      </script>

  </head>

  <body onclick="closer()" >
    <H1>Drop-down menus</H1>

    <input type = "text" onfocus="this.value=''" onclick="closer()">
    <br>
    <input id = "textField" type = "text"
      name = "textField" onkeyup = "handler()">

      <div id = "targetDiv"  onblur="closer()"></div>
  </body>
</html>
```

124

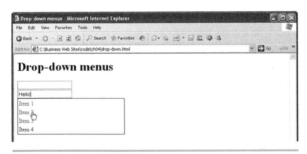

Figure 4-21   drop-down.html

You can see the results in Figure 4-21. The drop-down menu that appears is really just an HTML table of hyperlinks without underlines that appears in a `<div>` element with an opaque background, and each link is connected to a JavaScript URL. Those URLs call JavaScript functions that display alert boxes indicating which menu item you clicked. You can see the alert box that appears if you click the second menu item in Figure 4-22.

Figure 4-22 Catching a menu
selection

As you can see, it's a lot of work doing the JavaScript for even a rudimentary menu system—if you want to add this kind of control to your web page and want professional results, take a look at using a JavaScript library like Dojo. Or consider adding prebuilt controls available in various web page design applications.

Site Design and Search Engine Optimization

This chapter gives you a good working knowledge of business web site design and search engine optimization (SEO).

SEO has become big business lately, because so many people want to be first in the search-engine results. But you don't have to pay big bucks—all you need to do is to read this chapter, which should improve your ranking. (However, if your site is on a highly competitive topic, you might need to invest in the help of a specialist after all.)

Start with a Plan

My strong recommendation is to start your business web site with a plan. I've seen too many people waste too much effort putting up terrific pages that had to be totally reworked as their sites grew.

Business web sites should focus on layout and navigation, topics we'll look at in overview first. Clean layouts and intuitive navigation are important to any business site. To facilitate navigation, I suggest using a menu bar of links at the bottom of every web page.

The basis of a web site is, of course, just a single page: the home page, shown here. Make sure it loads fast, and make it as visually appealing as you can.

Home page

Business web sites vary widely, of course, but a popular option is to have product web pages, one per offered product or service, and all accessible from the home page using links or menus of links:

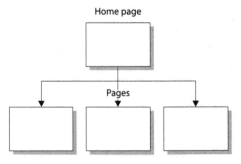

Now that you've started to give your web site some structure, here's an important point: when you attract customers by having them click on an ad (called a *click-through ad*), you can't just have them land on your home page. Instead, make sure they land on the page that covers the product they're looking for. The page they land on after clicking an ad is called the *landing page*.

The landing page should draw users into the product or service they're looking for. If you're advertising widget A and users have come to you by clicking an ad, then the landing page should be all about widget A—not a general page about the wonderful world of widgets that makes users hunt for the information they want. Remember, web users have notoriously short attention spans—if they have to think, chances are you've lost them.

Many business sites also have a shopping cart and checkout section, accessible from the product or service pages:

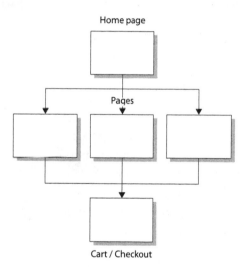

And many business sites let you search from the home page or any product page for other product pages, as shown in the following illustration:

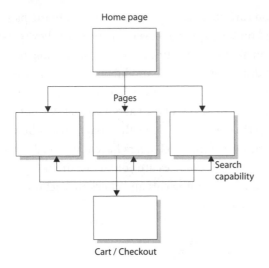

Home page

Pages

Search capability

Cart / Checkout

In addition, it's a good idea to have a contact page (see illustration below), even if it's just a collection of mailto: URLs, which run the risk of being harvested by robots and added to spam mailing lists, and not those more snazzy e-mail forms (see Chapters 9 and 10). It's also essential to have a help page or system, even if it's just a Frequently Asked Questions (FAQ) list. I really dislike sites that have no help system and tell users to post questions on their "user forum." It gives the impression they don't care about you, and even in the best case, there'll be a delay of days before you get an answer. I almost always find the advice I get to be worthless.

That's the layout of a basic business web site. Yours could be more, or less, complex, but these elements are very familiar to web surfers; they'll expect them when doing business with any substantial company. Some business sites have hundreds of thousands—even millions—of web pages (think Amazon), of course, and many more elements are available. Here's a list of the page elements you'll commonly find on business sites. When you're designing your site, take a look at this list to see that you've included all the pages you need:

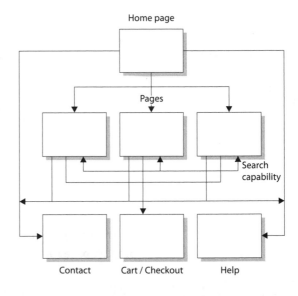

Home page

Pages

Search capability

Contact   Cart / Checkout   Help

- Home
- Product/service—Landing
- Contact Us
- Product Detail Description
- Shopping Cart
- Checkout
- Order Status
- About Us
- Frequently Asked Questions (FAQ)
- Help
- Community Forum/Feedback
- Preferences
- Site Map
- For the Media (press releases and contacts)
- Survey (to keep in touch with your customers)
- Shareholders
- RSS Signup
- Privacy Policy
- Copyright
- Bios of Personnel
- Driving Directions
- Calendar of Upcoming Event
- Job Opportunity

Business Page Design Principles

Okay, you've laid out an overall plan of your web site; it's time to create your pages. The actual design of your pages is up to you, but I'll make some general suggestions. One important tip before we start: check your pages in multiple browsers (at least Internet Explorer and Firefox), with multiple screen resolutions—and, if you can, on multiple platforms (Windows, Mac OS, and so on). The results will surprise you.

Business pages should be attractive, fast loading, appealing, center on content and not gimmicks, and have a strong visual focus (not a lot of disparate elements). Avoid very complex designs.

Here are some general suggestions—if you disagree with a suggestion, just ignore it—I know these are a matter of taste:

- Use a white or light pastel background.
- Keep a uniform theme throughout the site.

- Place the company logo on every page.

- Don't use text on top of a multicolored background that it blends into or clashes with—taupe on top of brown is bad news, for example.

- Use dark text on light backgrounds, which is easier on the eyes than light text on dark backgrounds.

- Avoid too much animation and, unless you really want it, music that starts by itself when the page loads.

- Do not use pop-ups, or keep them to a minimum.

- Keep image sizes small—you can get graphics programs that reduce the number of colors used, and so on—to make the images load faster.

- Avoid too many frames. Using two is okay if you need them.

- Don't expect the user's browser to have weird fonts installed—if you want to use obscure fonts, instead embed an image with the text.

- Use the same font throughout your site.

- Make sure your page will work in multiple browsers.

- If you use advanced technology in your site, make sure your pages still work well with people who have older browsers.

- Use width and height attributes for images—not only will your page load faster, but also the page won't squirm around as the browser displays the images.

- Make sure you have consistent navigation on each page, such as a navigation bar of links that appears at the bottom of every page. At least have a Home link or button on every page.

- Have a site map available—not only is this good for your customers, it's good for search engine robots.

- Take a look at your competitors' sites—learn from and improve on them (don't just copy).

■ Don't use copyrighted material without permission—millions of sites do, but sometimes it turns around and bites you.

You might want to keep in mind the "three-click rule," which says that ideally, any content on your site should only be a maximum of three clicks away. That's not always possible, but will make your site easy to navigate, with no annoying unnecessary sites. I use a nutrition site that takes you through 17—yes, 17—pages to check out once your shopping cart is ready; needless to say, that's needless.

Using HTML Editors and Templates

To actually construct your pages, I suggest you use the HTML expertise you gained from Chapters 1 and 2. However, you can also use HTML editors or prebuilt templates. I avoid these, because sooner or later (usually sooner), I always run into something I want to do that's not possible with these tools.

We saw a table of available HTML editors in Chapter 1; here it is again in Table 5-1 for reference.

Amaya	Aptana	Arachnophilia	Blaze Composer
Bluefish	CoffeeCup HTML Editor	Contribute	Dreamweaver
Evrsoft First Page	FrontPage	Freeway	GoLive
HomeSite	HTML-Kit	KompoZer	Microsoft Expression Web
Mozilla Composer	Nvu	Quanta Plus	RapidWeaver
SeaMonkey Composer	Serif WebPlus	TrellianWebPage	Virtual Mechanics SiteSpinner
WebCreator	Website X5	Web Studio	

Table 5-1   Some HTML Editors

133

I've heard good things about these free HTML editors:

- PageBreeze   www.pagebreeze.com/

- Nvu   www.nvu.com/

- BlueVoda   www.bluevoda.com/

- Trellian WebPage   www.trellian.com/webpage/

- Google Page Creator (web based)   http://pages.google.com/

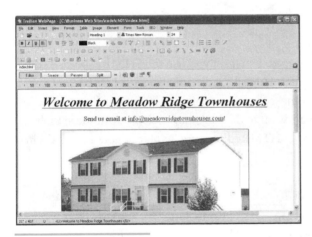

The free HTML editor I've heard the best things about is Trellian WebPage, which you can see at work in Figure 5-1, editing the sample web page we developed in Chapter 1. It's an easy WYSIWYG (what you see is what you get) editor.

Instead of starting your web pages from scratch, you can also work from preexisting web pages or templates. You can always view the HTML behind web pages in a browser by using the browser's View menu (such as View | Source). Or you could import existing pages using the File | Import Page menu item in Trellian WebPage.

Figure 5-1   Trellian WebPage at work

Here are some sites that offer free web page templates:

- www.freewebsitetemplates.com/
- www.steves-templates.com/
- http://freesitetemplates.com/
- www.freewebtemplates.com/

You can also buy more sophisticated web page templates online at sites like these:

- www.websitetemplates.name/
- www.templatemonster.com/
- www.wcbsitetemplates.com/
- www.top1000templates.com/

Search Engine Optimization

Now we'll get into a topic that is very popular as well as fascinating—search engine optimization (SEO). The goal of SEO is to get your site high up in the search results of major browsers. Since about 85 percent of Internet traffic is driven by search engine results, that's no mean topic.

SEO is a fascinating subtopic of a larger fascinating topic—marketing on the Internet. The Internet is a crowded place, and making your business stand out can be difficult. Some businesses develop sites as an auxiliary to their storefront business, and for them, standing out on the Internet is not as crucial. But if your business is Internet reliant, standing out becomes very important. You have two main ways to approach standing out and driving customers to your site—advertising and SEO. Advertising such as pay-per-click advertising is becoming increasingly expensive, and many hopeful Internet businesses are finding it just doesn't make economic sense anymore. To bid for clicks on even a modestly popular keyword these days can easily cost $5 per click in Google AdWords, and unless you make a lot of money per customer (typically not the case for Internet businesses, where customers often expect everything to be free), that's bad news. My own belief is that the majority of pay-per-click advertisers who are trying to make money solely from the Internet are losing money these days.

The other main option is SEO—that is, making your site rise in search engine result lists for free—so that surfers will click on and navigate to your site. The Internet truly is a crowded place, however, so if you're relying on SEO and the Internet for most of your income, you absolutely must find a niche (where there's less competition) and target it. What niche will work for you? We'll discuss that more in the next chapter, but you'd probably be surprised at how small niches can work for you.

SEO is all about optimizing your search rank based on a keyword or set of keywords that the user enters into the search engine. So you start the process with a site or a page and a keyword or a set of keywords, then optimize your page or site for those keywords. But if you've thought about what the right keyword is for your SEO and can't come up with anything, how can you find the right keyword?

Online Keyword Suggestion Tools

Plenty of tools can suggest keywords. All the major pay-per-click sites—Google, Yahoo, MSN, and so on—have built-in tools that will suggest keywords for you. You type in the keyword you have in mind, and the keyword suggestion tool comes up with all kinds of similar keywords to consider. Remember, SEO is all about optimizing your web page or site for specific keywords, so how you tune your pages depends on what keywords you select. Here are some online keyword suggestion tools, if you want to give them a try:

- https://adwords.google.com/select/KeywordToolExternal

- http://freekeywords.wordtracker.com/

- http://tools.seobook.com/keyword-tools/seobook/

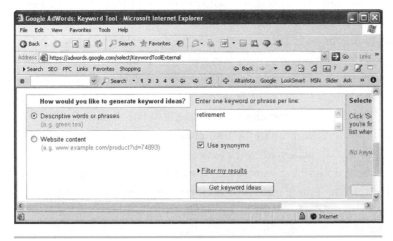

Figure 5-2   Using the Google keyword suggestion tool

A good keyword suggestion tool, such as Google's, at https://adwords.google.com/select/KeywordToolExternal, will tell you what kind of search volume you can expect to get by using given keywords. I'm using Google's keyword suggestion tool in Figure 5-2 to search for suggestions for the keyword "retirement." You can see how many searches were made on that keyword and Google's other suggestions in Figure 5-3.

As you can see in Figure 5-3,

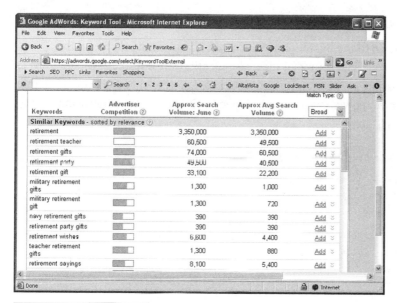

Figure 5-3   Keyword suggestion and traffic results

"retirement" is a wildly popular keyword—and I'd advise staying away from such keywords if you're a small business trying to earn a living on the Internet. Probably too many big-time players will be competing with you to let you rise to the top in the rankings.

An informal way of checking for a viable niche is to enter a candidate keyword into Google and to take a look at the number of paid ads that appear at right and on top of the search results. Paid ads are there because people have often given up on SEO due to competition, and they want to attract your attention. You want some paid ads, but not too many—too many means the niche is closed. A couple paid ads are fine, but the keyword "retirement" has a staggering 874 paid ads—indicating that there's too much competition for you to make a dent on Google unless you spend huge amounts of money per click. The amount of intense competition indicates that "retirement" is not a good candidate for SEO if you are relying on the Internet as the sole source of your income (unless you make something like an average of $10 or more for every person who views your site). The keyword "wedding toasts," which has proved a viable niche for some people, has four paid ads. You may want more than that, or you may want fewer—you've got to experiment.

Desktop Keyword Suggestion Tools

You can also take a look at the desktop keyword suggestion tools, such as those from www.wordtracker.com/ and www.webceo.com. Keyword suggestion tools are often part of the desktop SEO applications that we'll look at later in this chapter.

How to Do SEO

Let's get down to the business of SEO. Even if you're not relying on the Internet as your sole source of income, you still want your page or site to be as high as possible in the search engine results. Let's look at how to do SEO and then optimize the web page we developed in Chapter 1, townhouses.html, to show how it's done:

```
<html>
  <head>
    <title>
      Meadow Ridge Townhouses
    </title>
  </head>

  <body bgcolor="#fffff5">
    <center>
      <h1><i><u>Welcome to Meadow Ridge Townhouses</u></i></h1>
      Send us email at <a href =
        "mailto:info@meadowridgetownhouses.com?subject=Rentals">
        info@meadowridgetownhouses.com</a>!
      <br>
      <br>
      <img src="triplex.jpg" width="600" height="339"
        border="1" alt="townhouse">
      <br>
      <br>
      <table border="1" cellspacing="8">
        <tr>
          <td><img src="side.jpg" width="461" height="383"
            alt="side"></td>
          <td><img src ="chairs.jpg" width="476" height="384"
            alt="chairs"></td>
        </tr>
      </table>
      <br>
      These beautiful townhouses are only four years old, and feature
      a luxurious interior. Each of the townhouses in each of the
      five buildings is large (about 1600 square feet), quiet, has
```

```
      three floors, two to three bedrooms, two bathrooms, walk-in
      closet, finished basement, refrigerator, stove, dishwasher,
      and outside deck. The insides are very sharp; lawn maintenance
      and snow plowing are included. They're in a beautiful setting.
    <br>
    </center>
    <hr>
    <center><i>&copy; 2008 Meadow Ridge Townhouses</i></center>
  </body>
</html>
```

Because Google and the other search engines don't release their algorithms for determining page ranking, SEO is something of an art. Also, keep in mind that although SEO makes pages more appealing to the search engine robots ("spiders") that scan the Internet, your pages are really targeted to people, not robots. Here are my rules for SEO:

- Place your keywords in a `<meta>` element with the `name` attribute set to `"keywords"`. Complete information on creating `<meta>` elements is coming up in the next section in this chapter. Separate your keywords with commas. Each keyword can actually be multiple words, such as "townhouse living." You are allowed 1000 characters of keywords, and you should use most of them.

- Place a description of your page in a `<meta>` element with the `name` attribute set to `"description"`. Complete information on creating `<meta>` elements is coming up in the next section in this chapter. You are allowed 250 characters of description, and you should use most of them. Do not just stuff keywords here, which search engines don't like—use natural language.

- Use some of your keywords—the ones you consider the most important—in your `<title>` element (inside the `<head>` element). The most important keyword should start at character 1 in the text in the `<title>` element. Also use the keywords you use in the `<title>`

element in the `<body>` element, or the search engine may suspect you of "keyword stuffing" your `<title>`.

■ Use at least five of your keywords in the `<body>` of your page, but don't have too many keyword occurrences (known as "keyword spamming"—an SEO application can tell you if you have too many keyword occurrences in the `<body>`).

■ Sites that have multiple pages linked to each other do better in the rankings. Make sure all your pages are accessible via links so robots can find them.

■ For multipage sites, link to your other pages, and use keywords in the text of each link (for example, `<a href="xxx">keyword keyword keyword</a>`).

■ Search engines give great importance to seeing if other pages and sites link to yours. This is of primary importance for your rank—if more people link to your page, search engines will consider your page more important. Do not, however, sign up for "link farms," which host links just to fool search engines—the search engines have gotten wise to such tricks. The sites that link to yours should be relevant to yours.

■ The earlier you use keywords in your `<body>` element, the better (starting at character 1 is best). You should put some of your keywords in the `<body>` element in bold with the `<b>` element. Coloring them red using a `<font>` element is also good.

■ Consider using the text from your `<title>` element (which is displayed in the search results) in the first `<h1>` header in your page— which tells the search engine people who click your listing in their search results that they've come to the right place.

■ Do not use the same word-for-word title on different pages in your site. Your pages might look the same to the search engine and be considered as one page.

- Do not create robot-only pages (called *doorway pages*); search engines will lower your rank if you do.

- Include keywords in the `alt` attribute of `<img>` elements (the `alt` text is displayed when you hover the mouse over an image). This is very important.

- If you have a top or left navigation bar of links, consider using text links that the search engine can read instead of, or in addition to, images. Otherwise, the search engine may think your actual keyword-rich content starts too late in the page.

- Make sure your site or page loads quickly—if it times out, it won't be indexed.

- Avoid too much PDF—not all search engine robots can read PDF. Google is a notable exception.

- Use the hyperlink `<a>` element's `title` attribute to add descriptive text to your links, and use keywords in those titles. This is like adding keywords to the `alt` attribute of an `<img>` element.

- To create links to your site that the search engine robots will see, consider creating a blog and linking to the pages on your site. And keep the blog up to date.

- Include a site map (and a link to it on the home page, and perhaps on all pages), and make sure the site map includes an easy link trail to get to every location on your site.

- If you're going to use HTML comments, make sure you use some of your keywords in them.

- Select a domain name that includes your most important keyword or two.

- Stick with text and graphics as much as possible, and don't get too fancy—search engines can't read Flash, for example, so you should probably limit the use of Flash.

- Make sure all web pages in your site have links to the site's Home page.

- Include Copyright and About Us pages on your site.

- Don't use hidden or invisible text in an effort to cram more keywords into a page. Search engines will penalize your ranking for this tactic.

- Use a different order for your keywords in the body of a page, not the same order as in the <meta> elements.

- Avoid the use of text on a page's background.

- Do not submit identical pages that use different URLs.

- Validate your HTML to make sure search engine robots can read it.

- Consider using CSS style sheets for the display aspects of your page—search engine robots seem to like that, because all the display aspects of your page have been removed from the content, making the content more accessible.

That's the SEO list from the viewpoint of a search engine robot. Want to see your page as a search engine robot would? Try loading it into a text-only browser such as Lynx. If there is too much extraneous material before the actual content of your page starts, take that as a warning.

Link Google and Yahoo allow you to use a robots.txt file, which is XML, to let their robots index your site more quickly and completely. See the details at http://www.robotstxt.org/robotstxt.html.

Using <meta> Elements

HTML <meta> elements are important for SEO, because such elements let you give the search engine the keywords you want to be connected to, and the description of your page. Here are the attributes of the <meta> element:

- **content** Required attribute giving the content of a *name=value* pair. The actual value you use depends if you're using the name or the http-equiv attribute.

- **dir**   Gives the direction of directionally neutral text (text that doesn't have inherent direction in which you should read it). Possible values: LTR: left-to-right text or table, and RTL: right-to-left text or table.

- **http-equiv**   Connects the `content` attribute to an HTTP header field. If a browser asks for the page, the value of the `content` attribute will be passed to the browser as part of the HTTP header.

- **id**   Unique alphanumeric identifier for the tag, which you can use to refer to it.

- **lang**   Base language used for the tag.

- **name**   Connects the `content` attribute to a name, such as "Keywords." When a web browser or other agent requests the data connected to the name, the value of the `content` attribute will be sent.

- **scheme**   Specifies a predetermined format to be used to interpret the `content` attribute value.

To tell the search engine what keywords your page should be found under, set the `<meta>` element's `name` attribute to `"keywords"`, and assign the words and phrases, separated by commas, in a single text string to the `content` attribute (you have 1000 characters):

```
<meta name="keywords" content="keywords, separated by commas,
  can be words or phrases">
```

You should also add a human-readable description to your web page with the `name` attribute set to `"description"` and assign the `description` string—up to 250 characters—to the `content` attribute:

```
<meta name="description" content="Here is the description of my
  Web page, it is a great page.">
```

You can also force the browser to refresh the current page after a few seconds this way. It refreshes the current page after 5 seconds, for example, when you're creating a chat room and want to refresh the display with what others have been typing:

```
<meta http-equiv="refresh" content="5">
```

Or this way, which redirects the browser after 5 seconds to a new URL:

```
<meta http-equiv="refresh" content="5;url=newURL">
```

Okay, now we know all about SEO. Let's see an example.

SEOing an Example

We'll SEO townhouses.html, our example from Chapter 1, which also appears earlier in this chapter.

Our main keyword will be `"townhouse"`, so we'll use that keyword in the page's title, starting at character 1 (that's important):

```
<html>
  <head>
    <title>Townhouse - Meadow Ridge townhouses - the luxury
    townhouse</title>
         .
         .
         .
```

Now let's tackle the keyword's `<meta>` element—that's a `<meta>` element with the `name` attribute set to `"keywords"` and the `content` attribute set to your keywords (I always do the main keywords first), separated by commas. Bear in mind that keywords can also be phrases. You have 1000 characters here, so make the most of it (don't repeat any keywords here):

```
<html>
  <head>
    <title>Townhouse - Meadow Ridge townhouses - the luxury
    townhouse</title>
    <meta name="keywords" content="townhouse, townhouses, apartments,
     houses, housing, townhouse living, townhouse lifestyle, spacious
     townhouse, spacious townhouses, off-street parking, deck, rental
```

```
townhouses, rental townhouse, townhouse life, rental living at
its finest, luxury rental, luxury rentals, lake view,
closest to mall, outdoor barbeque, lawn maintenance included,
three-level house, two-bathroom house, townhome, townhome
lifestyle, townhome life, spacious townhome, rental townhome,
luxury townhome">
            .
            .
            .
```

Next comes the description, which is a `<meta>` element with the `name` attribute set to `"description"` and the `content` attribute set to a human-readable description of your page. Descriptions can be up to 350 words, so make the most of that. Make sure your primary keyword is at character 1 of the description, and use at least three of your keywords in the description (don't use any one keyword more than six times):

```
<html>
  <head>
    <title>Townhouse - Meadow Ridge townhouses - the luxury
    townhouse</title>
    <meta name="keywords" content="townhouse, townhouses, apartments,
     houses, housing, townhouse living, townhouse lifestyle, spacious
     townhouse, spacious townhouses, off-street parking, deck, rental
     townhouses, rental townhouse, townhouse life, rental living at
     its finest, luxury rental, luxury rentals, lake view,
     closest to mall, outdoor barbeque, lawn maintenance included,
     three-level house, two-bathroom house, townhome, townhome
     lifestyle, townhome life, spacious townhome, rental townhome,
     luxury townhome">
    <meta name="description" content="Townhouse luxury for rent. This
      is the finest townhouse in the area, at a very good price. Live
      the good life in Meadow Ridge townhouses. This is in the top
      one percent of area housing">
  </head>
          .
          .
          .
```

In the `<body>` of your page, use at least five of your keywords, make sure keywords appear early on, and put some early ones in bold:

```html
<html>
  <head>
    <title>Townhouse - Meadow Ridge townhouses - the luxury
    townhouse</title>
    <meta name="keywords" content="townhouse, townhouses, apartments,
     houses, housing, townhouse living, townhouse lifestyle, spacious
     townhouse, spacious townhouses, off-street parking, deck, rental
     townhouses, rental townhouse, townhouse life, rental living at
     its finest, luxury rental, luxury rentals, lake view,
     closest to mall, outdoor barbeque, lawn maintenance included,
     three-level house, two-bathroom house, townhome, townhome
     lifestyle, townhome life, spacious townhome, rental townhome,
     luxury townhome">
    <meta name="description" content="Townhouse luxury for rent. This
      is the finest townhouse in the area, at a very good price. Live
      the good life in Meadow Ridge townhouses. This is in the top
      one percent of area housing">
  </head>

  <body bgcolor="#fffff5">
    <center>
      <h1><i><u>Welcome to Meadow Ridge Townhouses</u></i></h1>
      Send us email at <a href =
        "mailto:info@meadowridgetownhouses.com?subject=Rentals">
        info@meadowridgetownhouses.com</a>!
      <br>
      <br>
      <img src="triplex.jpg" width="600" height="339"
        border="1" alt="townhouse">
      <br>
      <br>
      <table border="1" cellspacing="8">
        <tr>
          <td><img src="side.jpg" width="461" height="383"
            alt="apartment exterior"></td>
          <td><img src ="chairs.jpg" width="476" height="384"
            alt="apartment interior"></td>
        </tr>
```

```
      </table>
      <br>
      <b>These beautiful townhouses</b> are only four years old, and
      feature a luxurious interior. Each townhouse in each of
      the five buildings is large (about 1600 square feet), quiet,
      has three floors, two to three bedrooms, two bathrooms, walk-in
      closet, finished basement, refrigerator, stove, dishwasher,
      and outside deck. The insides of each townhouse are very sharp;
      lawn maintenance and snow plowing are included. They're in a
      beautiful setting--this is a townhouse for fine living. Come
      live the townhouse lifestyle here.
      <br>
    </center>
    <hr>
    <center><i>&copy; 2008 Meadow Ridge Townhouses</i></center>
  </body>
</html>
```

And there you have it—townhouses.html SEO'd.

Use SEO Software

There's also SEO software available that will tune your web pages. Let's take a look at that.

Desktop Software

Here are a couple of desktop SEO programs that you can buy:

- www.webceo.com

- www.seoelite.com/index2.htm

- www.ibusinesspromoter.com/

- www.webpositiongoldpro.com/

I'm not too enchanted with stand-alone SEO software. I've used Web CEO, and although I've gotten some good results with it, I've found it very difficult to use.

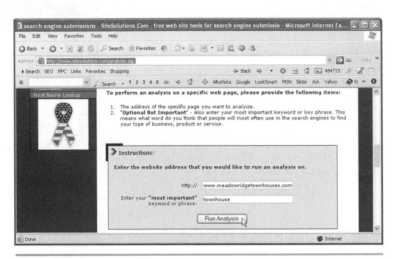

Figure 5-4   SiteSolutions

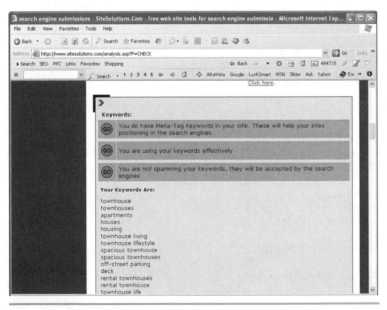

Figure 5-5   SEO report part 1

Online Software

Here are some free online SEO programs:

- www.websiteoptimization.com/ services/analyze/

- www.sitesolutions.com/ analysis.asp

- http://mikes-marketing-tools .com/ranking-reports/

My favorite is SiteSolutions— it's powerful and easy to use. Let's check townhouse.html using this program, as you can see in Figure 5-4, where we're checking the keyword "townhouse."

The results appear in Figures 5-5 to 5-7. As you can see, we're getting the (green) "GO" light. Cool.

Use a SEO Company

You can also use an SEO company to boost your search engine ranking, but these companies are often expensive. Just search for "SEO" on Google. Here are a couple of possibilities (I haven't checked them out):

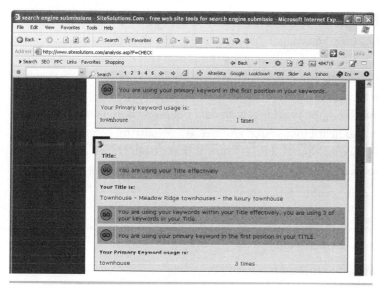

Figure 5-6   SEO report part 2

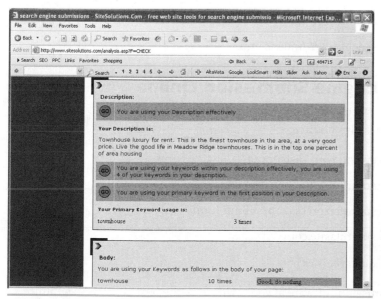

Figure 5-7   SEO report part 3

- www.sitesolutions.com/top3.asp

- www.submitexpress.com/
  optimize.html

Before engaging any such company, however, you should ask for a demonstration of their results. What sites have they helped? What are these sites' rankings?

Submit Your URL

When your new page or site has been tuned up, it's time to submit it to the search engines. Many submission services are out there, but this is something I think you should do yourself, as explained in the next section. Submit only once to search engines like Google, Yahoo, and MSN. Here are the URLs:

- www.google.com/addurl/

- https://siteexplorer.search
  .yahoo.com/submit

- http://search.msn.com.sg/docs/
  submit.aspx

Search Engine Submission Software

As I said, submitting your pages and sites to the search engines is something I believe you should do yourself. Some submission services say they'll submit your site to 500 search engines, but I have my doubts. There's no one-size-fits-all at the search engines, and the submissions will probably be a pretty poor fit to what the search engine is asking, with data fields left unfilled or incorrectly filled out. I've also heard that search engines are penalizing people who use submission services, although I don't know if that's true. Here's a starter list of site submission software you can download—some of this is not free:

- www.dynamicsubmission.com/
- www.trellian.com/seotoolkit/
- www.trellian.com/swolf/
- www.webceo.com/?source=Partners
- www.webpositiongoldpro.com/
- www.ibusinesspromoter.com/
- www.seoelite.com/index2.htm

Search Engine Submission Online

And here's a starter list of site submission software that you can use online—some of this is also not free:

- www.evrsoft.com/fastsubmit/
- www.addme.com/submission.htm
- www.submitexpress.com/submit.html
- www.submitasite.com/
- www.quickregister.net/

Use submission software at your own risk—the best policy is to submit your site yourself.

Marketing

In this chapter on Internet marketing (in addition to the SEO discussed in the previous chapter), we'll learn all about pay-per-click advertising, free advertising, e-mail lists, hit meters, and the like.

Let's start with a warning about pay-per-click advertising. This type of advertising has become vastly more expensive over the last ten years as more advertisers have crowded into the field. Many people are trying to make money on the Internet by selling low-cost items such as information (in the form of e-books and the like). Internet users are notoriously loath to part with their money, because there's a tradition and expectation that things on the Internet should be free.

So if you use pay-per-click advertising rather than SEO, you'll end up with a lot of clicks, but not necessarily a lot of sales. Don't let the bleeding get too bad. If you're losing money on pay-per-click advertising because people are clicking through to your site but just browsing and not buying, rethink. As mentioned, I believe that most people trying to make money exclusively from the Internet using pay-per-click advertising are losing money. Clicks have become fantastically expensive—it can cost $5 or more a click—and unless your surfers are buying expensive items and a lot of them, you very well may lose money.

Find a Niche

The most important aspect of Internet marketing is to find a niche. This doesn't apply if you've already got a physical business and just want to expand to the Internet, of course, but if you're going for Internet-only marketing, you have to find a niche, unless you're Wal-Mart. The Internet is so crowded that if your topic is too popular, you'll just be crowded off the search results page (remember, as mentioned in the example in Chapter 5, the keyword "retirement" had 872 paid ads). You have to find a niche and position your product to match that niche. For example, "get published" is too broad a topic (assuming you have an e-book on publishing). "Publish a nonfiction book" is too broad a topic. Even "publish a how-to book" is probably too broad. "Publish your diet book" might work.

Do Market Research

To find your niche, you have to do market research, and a lot of it. Use the keyword search tools discussed in Chapter 5 to get estimates of traffic for various keywords.

Check out your competition—take a look at the paid ads on Google for your keyword. You want some, but not a lot. You can also run surveys on social sites like Facebook (see the next chapter on how to do that).

Here's a guerilla marketing tactic you can try—a fake Buy button. It takes a lot of work to develop an e-book or a video course, or to import super-rare widgets. Some people do their market research with fake Buy buttons. They're just buttons labeled "Buy" that don't actually let the customer buy—because you don't have any product as yet—but instead record their click of that button. That way, you can compare your number of visitors to the number of purchases—called your *conversion rate*—before investing a lot of time and money developing a product that's not going to fly. You'll annoy some people this way, and you can probably kiss sales to them goodbye even if you're polite and ask them to come back later. Also note that just because someone clicks a Buy button doesn't mean they're actually going to buy—an appreciable fraction of people will opt out before entering any credit card information.

Another technique is to collect e-mail addresses to follow up regularly. It's been said that the same product has to be presented at least seven times to the average interested web surfer before they'll buy, and e-mail lists are perfect for that. For example, you may have a language tutoring site and sign people up on an e-mail list that promises them a word-a-day e-mail containing a common English word and its translation into four other languages. Promote your tutoring service in each e-mail (actually, sending one such e-mail a day is probably too much—word-a-week would be better). You'll see how to use an online service to set up your e-mail list later in this chapter.

Start with a Landing Page

You'll need a landing page to steer your customers to when they click your ad. This page is where the clickable link in the ad directs them, and your landing page should be direct and give them just what they want. That is, don't use your company's home page if it's going to make the customers search for what they want. We'll use our townhouses page as our landing page in this chapter, and you can see that page in Figure 6-1.

The landing page should also have a call to action in it—an Add To Cart button, for example, or at least a phone number. We'll add the following call to action in our townhouses page—a message that the customer should call the property manager to arrange a showing:

Figure 6-1 The landing page

```
<!DOCTYPE html PUBLIC "-//W3C//DTD HTML 4.01 Transitional//EN"
http://www.w3.org/TR/html4/loose.dtd">
<html>
  <head>
    <title>
      Meadow Ridge Townhouses
    </title>
```

```
        </head>

<body bgcolor="#fffff5">
  <center>
    <h1><i><u>Welcome to Meadow Ridge Townhouses</u></i></h1>
    Send us email at <a  href =
      "mailto:info@meadowridgetownhouses.com?subject=Rentals">
      info@meadowridgetownhouses.com</a>!
    <br>
    <br>
    <img src="triplex.jpg" width="600" height="339"
      border="1" alt="townhouse">
    <br>
    <br>
    <table border="1" cellspacing="8">
      <tr>
        <td><img src="side.jpg" width="461" height="383"
          alt="side"></td>
        <td><img src ="chairs.jpg" width="476" height="384"
          alt="chairs"></td>
      </tr>
    </table>
    <br>
    These beautiful townhouses are only four years old, and feature
    a luxurious interior. Each of the townhouses in each of the
    five buildings is large (about 1600 square feet), quiet, has
    three floors, two to three bedrooms, two bathrooms, walk-in
    closet, finished basement, refrigerator, stove, dishwasher,
    and outside deck. The insides are very sharp; lawn maintenance
    and snow plowing are included. They're in a beautiful setting.
    <br>
    <br>
    <i><b>Give the property manager a call at 617.555.1212 today to
      arrange a showing!</b></i>
    <br>
    <br>
  </center>
  <hr>
  <center><i>&copy; 2008 Meadow Ridge Townhouses</i></center>
</body>
</html>
```

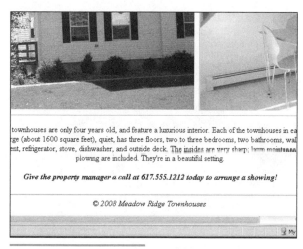

townhouses are only four years old, and feature a luxurious interior. Each of the townhouses in ea
rge (about 1600 square feet), quiet, has three floors, two to three bedrooms, two bathrooms, wal
ent, refrigerator, stove, dishwasher, and outside deck. The insides are very sharp; lawn maintenan
plowing are included. They're in a beautiful setting.

Give the property manager a call at 617.555.1212 today to arrange a showing!

© 2008 Meadow Ridge Townhouses

Figure 6-2 Call to action

You can see this call to action in Figure 6-2. This is a particularly low-key call to action, but in this case, we don't want huge, screaming, 48-point text, because these are luxury townhouses, and we want to appear civilized.

Craigslist

Let's start this chapter with a discussion of free, but still very effective, advertising on craigslist, www.craigslist.org. Currently (and there's no guarantee for the future, given how rapidly the Web evolves), craigslist is the best way to advertise anything that's restricted to a specific geographic location—such as townhouses.

Meadow Ridge Townhouses actually exist (they're beautiful places, should you be interested!), and I advertise them exclusively on craigslist. I've tried all sorts of ways to advertise—Google AdWords, local newspapers, sites for rentals and housing, but none of them comes close to craigslist—and it's free (as of this writing, anyway; some ad categories in some cities have a charge).

Craigslist is much like classified advertising in newspapers. You can post your ad for a specific geographic location once every 48 hours, not more often. Don't try to get around that by posting slightly different ads for the same thing more often than that. If the new ad is too similar, their automated software will pick it up and deny the listing—and if it doesn't, they might pick up the duplicate ad by visually scanning, and you run the risk of being banned. Craigslist is only for things limited to a specific geographic area (currently). If you post the same or a similar ad on multiple city sites, craigslist will ban you.

Go to www.craigslist.org now, and click the city you're interested in. If you don't see it, click the state and then the city (if your city doesn't appear, you can suggest that craigslist add it). You can see the Boston craigslist in Figure 6-3.

Meadow Ridge Townhouses are housing, so click the "apts/housing" link

155

MEMO

Besides using your e-mail address, there's nothing to stop you from placing phone numbers or links to landing pages in your listings.

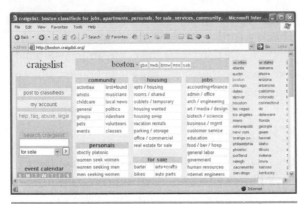

Figure 6-3   The Boston craigslist

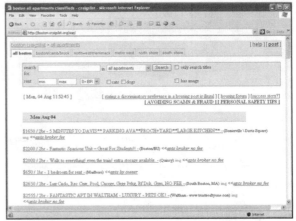

Figure 6-4   Apartments on Boston craigslist

156

under the "housing" heading to scope out the competition, which appears in Figure 6-4.

Clicking one of the links you see in Figure 6-4 brings up the listing's ad, as you see in Figure 6-5. Note the reply-to e-mail address—that's how potential customers get in touch with you.

The process of posting your own ad differs by what category you want to post and what city you're posting in. To get an idea, click the [post] link you see in Figure 6-4 at upper right, bringing you to the page you see in Figure 6-6.

Click "I am offering housing" to bring up Figure 6-7.

THE EASY WAY

Note that some of the listings in Figure 6-4 include the keyword "img," meaning an image is available in the ad. The other option is "pic"—"img" means an image referenced through an <img> element, and "pic" means an image you upload to craigslist. I recommend that you have images, of course, but that you write your ad using HTML and <img> elements to reference your images (as hosted on your ISP) rather than uploading images to craigslist. Uploaded images are reduced and appear only at the end of the listing, while images embedded with <img> elements are full size and can appear anywhere in the ad. Write your ad in HTML, rather than plain text. HTML allows you to style it to make more of an impression—you'll get better results. Note that craigslist is currently considering restrictions on what HTML elements you can use.

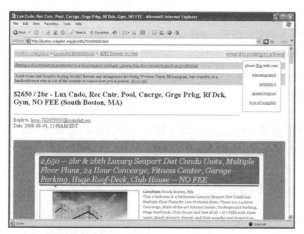

Figure 6-5   An apartment ad

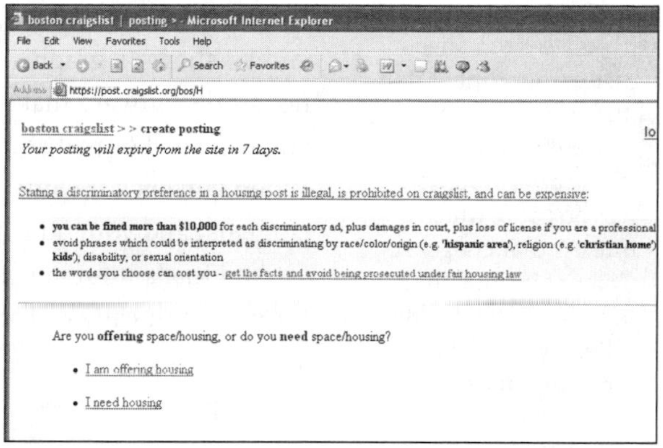

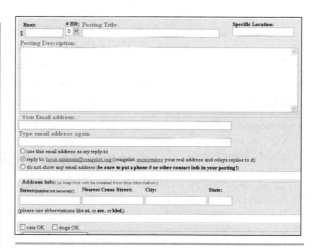

Figure 6-6   Posting an apartment ad

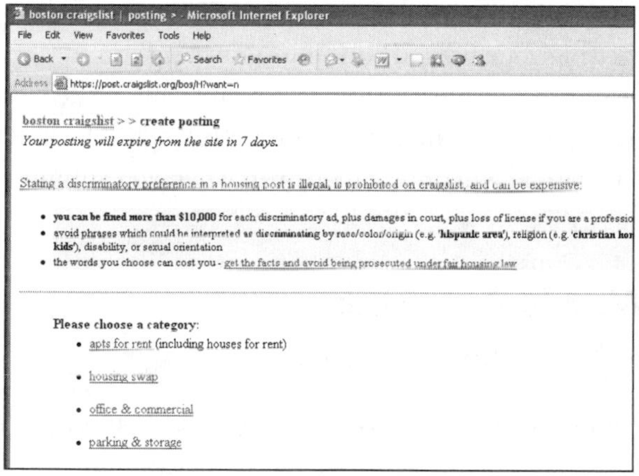

Figure 6-7   Selecting an apartment ad

Figure 6-8   Creating an apartment ad

157

Click "apts for rent" in Figure 6-7 to bring up the screen shown in Figure 6-8. This is where you create your ad. Fill in the rent, the number of bedrooms, the title you want displayed in the ad listing page, the text or HTML for your ad (in the Posting Description field), and your e-mail address. Then click Continue at the bottom of the page (off the screen in Figure 6-8).

When you click Continue, you'll be asked if you accept the terms of service, and be shown a graphic of some distorted text to type in (to make sure you're not some software that's automatically posting). When your ad is submitted, craigslist will e-mail you a link that you have to click to complete the process. When you click the link, your browser navigates to the ad acceptance page in craigslist and your ad is posted. Cool.

And that's it for craigslist—currently, you can't beat it for posting free ads for geographically restricted items.

Advertising on Google

When it comes to pay-per-click, Google is the big one. That doesn't necessarily mean it's the best one for your needs—it does almost always mean it's the most expensive one. Many people do advertise on Google, of course, and we'll take a look at the process here of signing up and getting your first ad running.

There are three steps to getting your first ad running, assuming you haven't done this before: you create a Google AdWords account, you create your first ad, and then you set up your billing information. We'll take a look at these steps here. Note that your ad will only actually run when you submit your billing information.

Create Your AdWords Account

First off, you have to create a Google AdWords account:

1. Go to the AdWords home page, http://adwords.google.com/select/.

2. Click the Click To Begin button.

3. Click the Standard Edition button.

4. Click Continue.

5. Click the appropriate button to indicate whether you have an existing Google Account.

6. Follow the instructions, entering your e-mail address and password.

7. Click Create Account (or Continue if you already have some type of Google account).

8. Select your currency.

9. Click Continue.

Okay, that gets your account started.

Your account will be activated once you've done two things: created your first campaign and entered your billing information.

Google will send you a welcome e-mail informing you that you can activate your account by creating your first "campaign" and by entering your billing information. The e-mail includes a link you should click: http://adwords.google.com. This takes you to a page where you can begin your campaign, as shown in Figure 6-9.

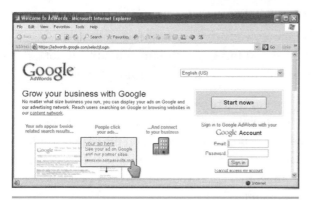

Figure 6-9   Here's where you start a campaign in the AdWord system.

Creating Your First Ad Campaign

Now it's time to create your first ad. Ads are stored in ad campaigns, and a campaign can have as many ads as you like. After you've signed into your AdWords account, here's how you create your first ad. (Google is always changing this process, so it might not be in the same order as you read here.)

1. Click the Create Your First Campaign button.

2. Select the language for the ad and geographic location targeting options (if any).

3. Click Continue.

4. Enter your ad's text in the form. You'll be asked for a headline for the

MEMO

Since you're creating your first ad here, you might want to look at some of the keyword suggestion tools discussed in the previous chapter. Don't forget to target your keyword to your niche. Always ask yourself what you'd type in if you were searching for your product. And bear in mind that users are much more likely to enter two- or three-word keywords rather than one.

ad, the body of the ad, the URL to display at the bottom of the ad, and the actual URL of the landing page (which can be different from the display URL).

5. Click Continue.

6. Enter keywords that will best target your ad when searched by Google users.

7. Click Continue.

8. Enter the amount of money you're willing to spend on this ad campaign each day. Note that this is a maximum amount—if not enough users click the ad, you won't reach this amount every day.

9. Enter the maximum amount you're willing to pay each time a user clicks your ad—this is called the CPC, or cost per click. Note: The CPC strongly influences the position of your ad on the search results page. The higher your bid, the higher your ad's position. This is also a maximum—if no competitor is near your price, you may not be charged the full CPC amount.

10. Click the View Traffic Estimator link to view your average CPC and cost estimates.

11. Click Continue.

12. Review all the information you've entered to create your first campaign. Click Edit if you want to change anything (doing so will return you to the edit pages).

13. Click Continue To Billing. The last step in getting started is to enter your billing information.

Enter Your Billing Information

Nothing actually happens with your ad until you enter your billing information. When you click Continue To Billing after setting up your first ad campaign, you'll be directed to the billing page. Here's what you do:

1. Enter your billing information.

2. Set the time zone for your account.

3. Agree to the AdWords terms and conditions.

4. Click Save and Activate.

That's all you need to do—your account should be up and running.

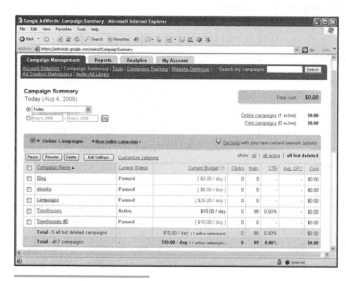

Figure 6-10 The Campaign Summary page

Working with Your Account

To work with your account in general, start by logging in at https://adwords.google.com/select/Login with the username and password you selected. (Google will remember your username and password when you've logged in this way for the next time you go to this page.) In the Campaign Management tab, click the Campaign Summary link. Doing so will bring up the Campaign Summary page you see in Figure 6-10.

The Campaign Summary is an overview of your ad campaigns. Remember, each campaign can have multiple ads in it. As you can see in Figure 6-10 in the Current Status column, campaigns can be either Active or Paused. Here are the columns you can see in Figure 6-10:

- **Campaign Name** The name of each campaign.

- **Current Status** Whether the campaign is active or paused.

- **Current Budget** The daily maximum you've budgeted for each campaign.

MEMO

To pause (stop running your ads) or resume a campaign, click the "Resume campaign" link you see in Figure 6-11 (which will read "Pause campaign" for active campaigns).

- **Clicks**   The number of users who've clicked any ad in your campaign today.

- **Impr(essions)**   The number of times the ads in the campaign have been displayed today.

- **CTR**   The click-through ratio (that is, Clicks/Impressions). You want to aim for at least 0.02 percent.

- **Avg CPC**   The average cost per click you're spending in the campaign.

- **Cost**   The total you've spent today.

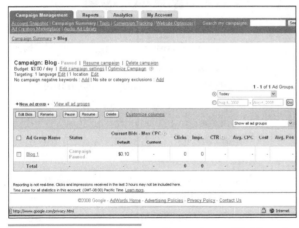

Figure 6-11   The Blog campaign

This is where you monitor your campaigns' performance. You watch the number of clicks and impressions—if you're not getting enough, it may be time to raise your keyword bids.

Let's take a look at a campaign—the Blog campaign, for example. Clicking the name of the campaign ("Blog") in Figure 6-10 opens the Blog campaign, as you see in Figure 6-11.

Each campaign is composed of as many ads as you want, and the ads in each campaign are organized into *groups*. The Blog campaign only contains one ad group, Blog 1, as you can see in Figure 6-11. Clicking the name of the ad group, Blog 1, opens its web page, as you see in Figure 6-12.

You can see the ad in the table in Figure 6-12—there's just one in this group, and you can see the statistics on the ad in Figure 6-12.

Creating a New Ad

Want to put a new ad in the current ad group (and therefore into the current ad campaign)? Click the Create New Ad: Text Ad link that you see in Figure 6-12 to open the new page you see in Figure 6-13.

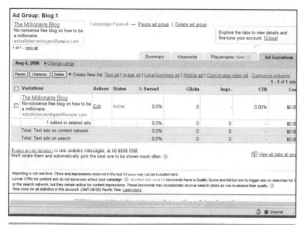

Figure 6-12   The Blog 1 ad group

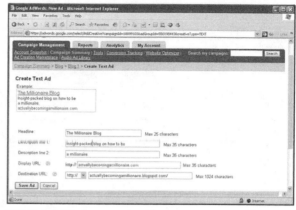

Figure 6-13   Creating a new ad

Here's how to create a new text ad:

1.   Fill in the headline in the Headline text field (max 25 characters).

2.   Fill in the Description Line 1 with the ad's text (max 35 characters).

3.   Fill in the Description Line 2 with the ad's text (max 35 characters).

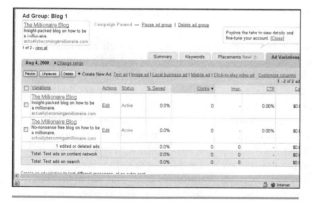

Figure 6-14   A new ad

4.   Add the Display URL; this URL will be displayed at the bottom of your ad.

5.   Fill in the Destination URL of the actual landing page.

6.   Click the Save Ad button. That adds the new text ad to the ad group, as you can see in Figure 6-14.

Want to add or change the keywords for an ad group? Click the Keywords tab you see in Figure 6-14, opening the page you see in Figure 6-15.

Figure 6-15   An ad group's keywords

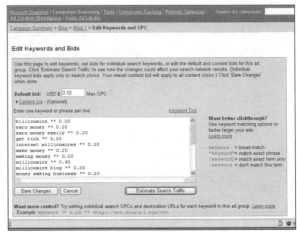

Figure 6-16   Editing an ad group's keywords

164

Note that in Figure 6-15, you can see the performance of each keyword in terms of impressions, clicks, and click-through ratio. This is where you tune your keywords' performance.

To make changes or to add keywords to an ad group, click the Edit Keywords link you see in Figure 6-15, opening the page you see in Figure 6-16.

As you can see in Figure 6-16, you can edit and add keywords for the

MEMO

The price you give to your click bids per keyword in Google AdWords is constantly being evaluated by Google. They may frequently decide it's not enough. I've had Google accept a $0.50 bid on a keyword, only to turn around the next day, deactivate the keyword, and demand a minimum of $0.80. After I gave it $0.80, some time later it deactivated the keyword again and demanded a minimum of $1. Curious, I gave it $1 per click for the keyword. Some time later,

it came back again and demanded $5 per click for the keyword. Needless to say, I left the keyword deactivated. It became a game—every day, I'd report to my wife how many keywords Google had deactivated and raised the price on, even when I hadn't touched the account, except to raise the bids as demanded by Google—"25 keywords today," "only 7 today," "whoops, 27 keywords today." How was I to plan an ad campaign when I spent a lot of time setting things

up, and then Google kept raising prices out of my reach over the next few weeks? The keywords they raised prices on were acceptable to them when I started, yet they started raising prices over time. What if I depended on my income from Google AdWords? I'd always have to live with the threat of suddenly being put out of business as Google raised its minimum acceptable click bids beyond my reach.

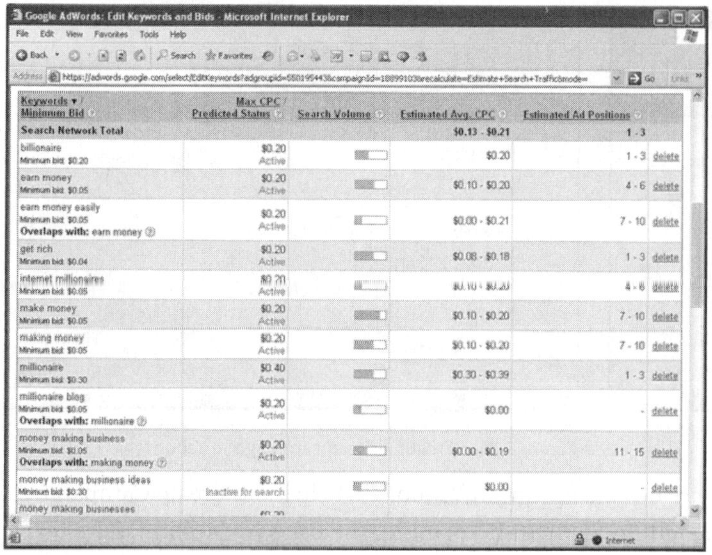

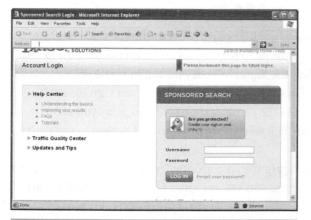

Figure 6-17   Estimating
keyword performance

current ad group here. When you click the Estimate Search Traffic button, Google shows you an estimate of search traffic by keyword, as you see in Figure 6-17.

Note that Figure 6-17 only gives you a relative estimate of search traffic, nothing like the detailed results you get with the Google keyword suggestion tool you saw in the previous chapter. What's good here, however, is the Estimated Ad Positions column, which gives you the level your ad will be at (if it's 4, for example, your ad will be below three others). Although this is just a rough estimate of ad position,

165

your keywords should usually be in the top ten positions if you want any clicks.

Advertising on Yahoo

Another popular pay-per-click advertiser is Yahoo, and I've always gotten the impression that it's less expensive than Google. You can sign up for an account at http://sem.smallbusiness.yahoo .com/searchenginemarketing/. Once you have a username and password, you can log in at https:// login21.marketingsolutions.yahoo.com/adui/ signin/loadSignin.do, as shown in Figure 6-18.

Signing into Yahoo marketing brings up your ad campaigns, as you can see in Figure 6-19.

Figure 6-18   Signing into Yahoo

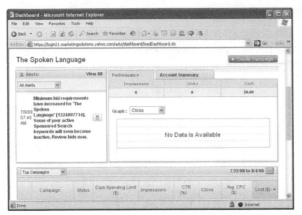

Figure 6-19   An ad campaign overview in Yahoo

Figure 6-20   Creating an ad campaign in Yahoo

How do you create a campaign in Yahoo? Just click the Create Campaign button at upper right in Figure 6-19, opening the page you see in Figure 6-20.

As you can see in Figure 6-20, the campaign-creation process is much the same as it is on Google. You create ad groups, connect them with keywords, set your bids, and so on. Just follow the links you see in Figure 6-20.

Advertising on MSN

Microsoft adCenter is another popular pay-per-click search engine, and you can advertise here as well—just go to https://adcenter.microsoft.com/ as you see in Figure 6-21, and click the Sign Up Today button to create an account.

When you've created a username and password, you can sign in, as shown in Figure 6-21. You're taken to the campaign overview page, as you see in Figure 6-22, where you can click your campaigns and ad groups to see their details.

Want to create a new campaign? Just click the Create Campaign button you see in Figure 6-22, and the page you see in Figure 6-23 appears. You're walked through the whole process: configuring the new campaign's settings, creating the ads, setting the keywords, and establishing the pricing.

MEMO

As you can see in the message at left in Figure 6-19, Yahoo, like Google, has the unfortunate habit of increasing the minimum bids on your keywords without warning. It's warning me that some of my keywords will soon become inactive. To me, this always has the feeling of raising the rent on a shopkeeper sporadically, without warning, after the shopkeeper has moved in.

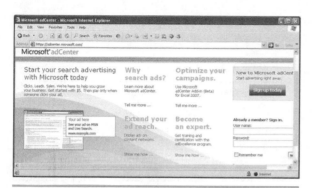

Figure 6-21   Signing into Microsoft adCenter

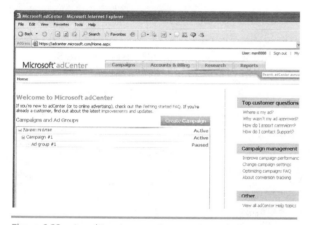

Figure 6-22   An adCenter campaign overview

Fundamentally, advertising in Microsoft adCenter is much like advertising on Google or Yahoo, although I got the impression that it's less expensive than the other two—for the moment, anyway.

Tracking Your Hits

When you're doing any marketing, keeping track of your metrics such as ad impressions, clicks, click-through ratio, and so on, is very important. Certainly, tracking your hits when you advertise on craigslist can help you tune your ads—if you make a change to your ad text, do the hits go up or down, for example?

But what about pay-per-click advertising? Don't they track the number of clicks on your ads, and so the number of people who end up on your landing page? Yes and no. My experience with pay-per-click advertising is that sometimes the number of clicks a search engine reports can be exaggerated. One site I was on routinely ran 30 percent higher in the number of clicks reported than what was measured on my landing page's hit counter. I asked about this and got a long, involved, complex, and entirely incomprehensible answer (what's a "super-cached" hit, anyway?). I thanked them politely and closed my account.

I've been using Site Meter at www.sitemeter.com/ to track the hits on my various landing pages. Site Meter appears in Figure 6-24.

The basic Site Meter service is free, although you can pay for more advanced metering. Just click the appropriate Sign Up! button as shown in Figure 6-24 and create an account. It's easy, and you'll get a snippet of HTML to embed in your landing page. Embedding that HTML draws a small Site Meter icon, as

167

Figure 6-23   Creating an adCenter campaign

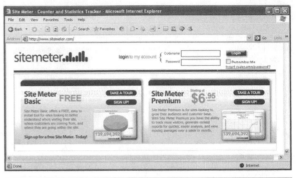

Figure 6-24   Site Meter

Figure 6-25   A Site Meter icon

shown in Figure 6-25, in your page and connects you to Site Meter.

Want to know your stats? Just click the Site Meter icon in your landing page, and you'll be taken to the page that tracks your hits on Site Meter, as shown in Figure 6-26.

As you see in Figure 6-26, Site Meter breaks down the clicks you've been getting by week, day, and even hour. A huge part of Internet marketing is tuning your ads, and Site Meter—which can also tell you where your users are coming from—can be a big part of that.

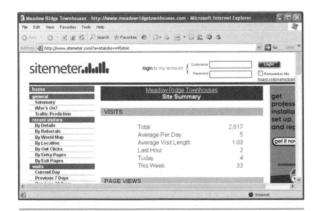

Figure 6-26   Site Meter stats

Using E-mail Lists

As I mentioned, it's conventional wisdom that for some types of products, users have to be exposed to them at least seven times before they'll buy. That's not true, obviously, of common items the user goes in search of—bandages at a drugstore site, for example—but it's often true of products you create yourself, such as online programming classes.

The strategy is to get people who come to your landing page to sign up for your e-mail list by offering them something of value. That could be a free report, a free sample, or something else of perceived value. The example I used earlier was for language training sites, where, to get people to sign up for your e-mail list, you offer them a daily or weekly word translated into four languages. I gave this a try, and a dozen people a day signed up.

The e-mail list management program I like is AWeber.com. It's powerful, cost-efficient (not free), and easy to work with. You write what you want your pop-up in your landing page to say to get people to sign up, and AWeber will give you the HTML to embed in your landing page—they handle the list from there.

You write the messages you want sent daily, weekly, or whatever, and set up the schedule as well. You can schedule according to the calendar, or according to when the person signed up (that is, even though you've been running your list for years, a newly signed-up person would get Message 1 first, Message 2 next, and so on). You can track how many people are on your e-mail list—and who they are.

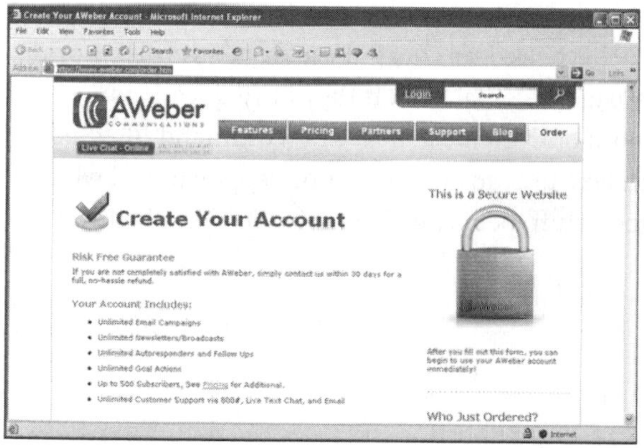

The AWeber people take great care to avoid spamming, but some of your recipients will inevitably complain to their ISP that you're spamming them (even though they signed up). That can be a problem if you get banned from, say, AOL, so AWeber does a spam score on your messages and warns you if there's a problem.

Want to sign up for this service? Go to www.aweber.com/order.htm, as you can see in Figure 6-27.

Figure 6-27   AWeber.com

Additional Thoughts on Marketing

Marketing on the Internet can be tough. If you have a super niche, things can go well—I've seen people become the sole importers of a certain type of Japanese novelty pen and make a living from those—but super niches can be hard to find.

It's important that you try to draw the users into your site as much as possible. In addition to asking them to sign up for your e-mail list with a tempting offer, you might set up a multipage tour of your products or services.

You can also give video tours or do a video presentation of your products or services (this can be particularly effective for services). Set up a streaming video. You shoot the video in WMV format and then upload it to a streaming video server (which costs money—the server I'd been using raised its prices a while ago and I closed my account). To find a server, just do an online search for "streaming video server." After you've signed up, you upload your WMV file, they give you its URL, and you link to that URL in your landing page. And now some special controls you can embed in your web pages let you do streaming video—take a look at www.aspnet-video.com/.

Another powerful technique is to offer free samples. If you are offering programming classes, for example, tell people that their first class is free.

And make it easy to get in touch with you if prospective customers have questions. Toll-free numbers have become cheap these days—at least provide people an e-mail address or page to contact you if they have questions.

Another way to get the word out? Create a blog—I recommend BlogSpot at www.blogspot.com. It can take time to attract a lot of people to read what you have to say, but if it's good stuff, people will show up (especially if you advertise).

Marketing on Facebook

Social networking sites have been garnering a lot of attention these days because of their overwhelming popularity—and their young demographic, which is desirable to marketers. This chapter covers the most promising of the social networking sites for marketers—Facebook. Facebook was originally created for college students, and although it's been broadened to accept anyone, it's still got an affluent clientele—and they've been opening up the site to marketers in a big way.

The caveat about marketing on social networking sites is that you have to be careful in presenting your message. Facebook members will ignore what they consider overt commercial content unless it's in one of the few marginally acceptable channels—clickable ads, for example. In fact, Facebook is littered with ways that users can label your messages as spam. If you send a message to people on your friend list, for example, and it seems too commercial, they can label your post "spam" with the click of their mouse—and that can ultimately get you banned from Facebook. So remember that on Facebook, users are in the driver's seat, not marketers. Instead of simply presenting commercial messages, you should strive for what's called *content marketing,* which means you have to draw people to you by providing interesting content.

MEMO

Marketing on Facebook is a big topic, and we don't have the space here to cover the entire topic in great depth. If you want more details, check out a good book on Facebook marketing.

What really provides a boost to Facebook marketing is the possibility of *viral marketing*, which means people who are excited about what you have to offer talk to each other and get others involved. Mark Zuckerberg, the founder of Facebook, says that in the last hundred years, "the way to advertise was to get into the mass media and push out your content." In the next hundred years, he says, "information won't be just pushed out to people, it will be shared among the millions of connections people have. Advertising will change. You will need to get into these connections."

Let's take a look.

Signing Up

The first step in working with Facebook is to sign up for your own account. To do that, go to www.facebook.com, as shown in Figure 7-1.

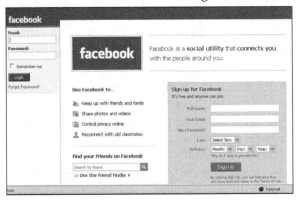

To sign up for an account, fill out the data in the box at right, and then click the Sign Up button. Facebook asks you all kinds of probing questions about your job, schools, demographics, and so on—if you don't want to answer a question, don't. It's notable that Facebook users have very little compunction about sharing very private data.

After you're set up, you can log in using your e-mail and password in the boxes at left in Figure 7-1.

Figure 7-1   Signing up for Facebook

Configuring Your Profile and Home Page

Logging in takes you to your home page—you can see mine in Figure 7-2.

The home page displays much information, including the *News Feed,* one of the most popular aspects of Facebook. The News Feed lets you track what your friends are doing; every time they do something, that news is posted to your News Feed.

Figure 7-2   My home page on Facebook

Figure 7-3   My Profile page on Facebook

Your public page is your *Profile page,* which you can see by clicking the Profile link shown in Figure 7-2. Your Profile page is visible to your friends, and you can see mine in Figure 7-3. The *Mini-Feed* is like the News Feed except that it holds information about what you've been doing. The Profile page also displays much of the information you gave Facebook when you signed up.

Facebook is heavily friend-oriented, and you can message people asking if they'll become your friend by clicking the "Send xxx a message" link under their photo in their profile (not visible in my profile in Figure 7-3, because I'm the one viewing it). You can organize your friends into friend lists and message (e-mail) them all at once, which is great for marketers.

Creating a Friends List

You can have up to 1,500 friends in a list—which is good for getting the word out. To make a new friend list, click the Friends link in your profile, and click the Make A New List button at right in the Friends page; then enter the name of the new list.

The next step is to add the friends you want in the new list. Here you can type the names of the friends you want to add—or you can select multiple friends at once by using the Select Multiple Friends link.

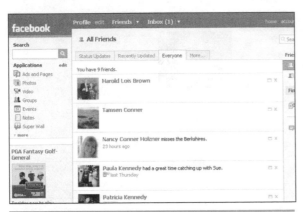

Figure 7-4   My friends on Facebook

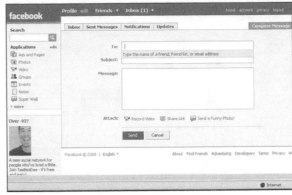

Figure 7-5   Messaging in Facebook

MEMO

Facebook needs to get credit card information from you before you can run a poll—each answer costs $0.25, and there's a $1 insertion fee. To connect a credit card to Facebook, click the Account link that appears at the top of all your Facebook pages, and enter your credit card information. Interestingly, the Account page often doesn't come up in Internet Explorer—it may for you, but I use Firefox to access my account information.

As you add new friends to the list, they appear on the page, as you see in Figure 7-4.

Now you can message everyone in a friend list by clicking the Inbox link you see in Figure 7-4, then clicking the Compose Message tab, as you see in Figure 7-5.

Messaging people on Facebook sends e-mail to their Inbox. You can enter the name of a friend list to send your message to, as indicated by the prompt you see in Figure 7-5.

Running a Poll

One of the good things about Facebook is that you can ask users what they want—it's a market researcher's dream. To create a poll, go to the Facebook Business Solutions page, http://www.facebook.com/business, as shown in Figure 7-6.

This is a page you should become familiar with if you want to market on Facebook—you can see links here to all the major marketing techniques on Facebook. Right now, we're interested in creating a poll, so click the Facebook Polls link, and click the Create A Facebook Poll button in the page that appears, opening the page you see in Figure 7-7.

Polls employ multiple-choice questions, so enter your question and answers.

Figure 7-6   The Facebook Business Solutions page

Figure 7-7   Creating a Facebook poll

175

You can also select the demographic you want to poll—sex, age, location, and so on. When you're ready, click the Continue button. Facebook shows you the details of your poll—click the Place Order button. Facebook will bring you to the results page of your poll—you can keep refreshing the page to see the results displayed as bar graphs. You also get a breakdown by age, sex, and so forth—great for market research.

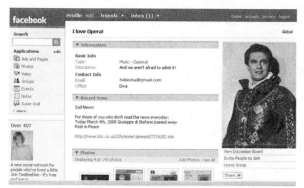

Figure 7-8   The I Love Opera! group page, top half

Working with Groups

One of the ways that Facebook members congregate—and so can rally around your brand—is on Facebook *groups*. There are thousands of groups on all kinds of interests—you can see the I Love Opera! (doesn't everyone?) group's page in Figure 7-8.

Groups include all kinds of ways for members to communicate with each other, such as a Discussion Board, which appears in Figure 7-9 for the I Love Opera! group.

You can join a group, or create your own group by clicking the Groups link at left in any of your Facebook pages, opening your Groups page, as shown in Figure 7-10.

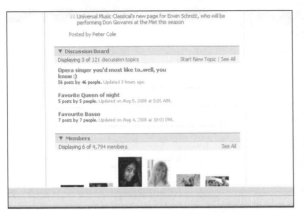

Figure 7-9   The I Love Opera! group page, bottom half

Figure 7-10   A Group page

You can browse through your existing groups by clicking the Browse Groups link, search for a group by entering a search term in the Search box, or create your own group by clicking the Create A New Group button, which opens the page you see in Figure 7-11.

Note the Network box in Figure 7-11. Facebook has set up hundreds of networks, and they're sort of like the tribe you belong to on Facebook. By default, you're added to your geographical area's network when you give your geographic data in creating your account. There are networks by geographic area, by school (including high schools), and by employer. You can see friend pages of others in your network, as well as other data that is hidden from people not in the same network.

Creating a group for your brand is easy—just fill in the fields and click the Create Group button. You can see a new group that I created as a demo, Beach Bum Rentals, in Figure 7-12.

Figure 7-11   Creating a group

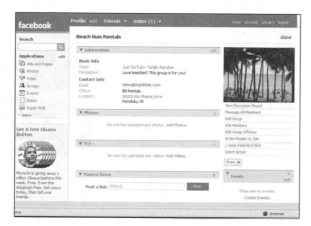

Figure 7-12   A new group

177

Creating a Page

Profile pages and friends are okay for small businesses, but what about larger
businesses or rock stars? A big-time CEO might not want to be bothered with
dozens of requests in his Inbox to become his Facebook friend every day.
(I hear that Bill Gates used to get something like 700 such requests a day.)

If Facebook profiles and friends are for individual people and very small
businesses, what do larger businesses do? They create a Facebook *page*. Pages
are designed for businesses and stars—average users can't become a friend of
a page, they become a *fan* instead. Fans can follow along with what's happening, and they can post to a page's discussion board (if you allow it), but not
more than that. They don't have the same privileges as friends to message
you, for example. However, as a page owner, you can message your fans en
masse.

To get started with pages, go to http://www.facebook.com/pages/, as you
see in Figure 7-13.

Here, you can search for pages by entering search terms and can browse
pages by type. For an example of a page, take a look at the Royal Opera House
page, shown in Figure 7-14.

Want to become a fan of the Royal Opera House? Just click the Become A
Fan link you see at upper right, which is present on all pages that allow fans.

Figure 7-13   Looking at Facebook Pages

Figure 7-14   The Royal Opera House page

Users can also share their favorite pages with their friends and—*voilà!*—viral marketing.

Okay, that's how pages look and work in overview—how can you create a page for your own business? To create a new Facebook page, you can go to http://www.facebook.com/pages/create.php, or simply click the Create A Page For Your Business link at the bottom of any existing Facebook page

MEMO

Getting to the page in Figure 7-13 becomes easier when you become a fan of a page or create your own page—a link named "Pages" will appear in the left navigation bar of all your standard Facebook pages.

(such as the Royal Opera House's page). Doing so brings you to the creation page you see in Figure 7-15.

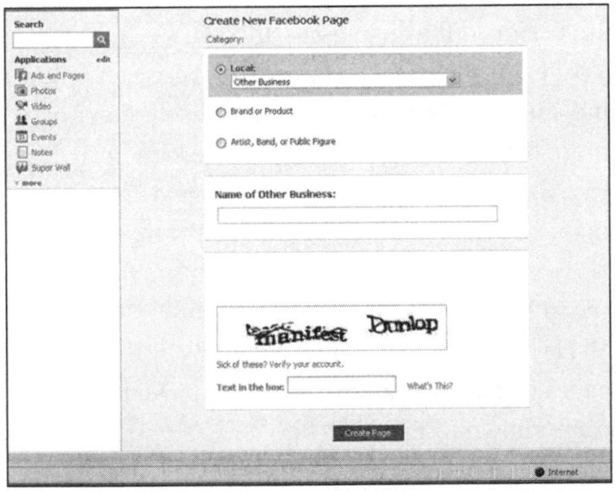

Enter the information to create your new page, click the Create Page button, and follow the directions. Among other things, you'll specify the administrators you want for the page, who are the

Figure 7-15   Creating a Facebook page

Figure 7-16   A new Facebook page

people allowed to make changes to the page.

If you're the creator or an administrator of a page, you'll see an Edit link (which regular users won't see) next to all sections of the page. You can click the link to make changes to the page. And that's how to create your own Facebook page.

For example, you can see a demonstration Facebook page I made for Meadow Ridge Town-houses in Figure 7-16.

Creating an Ad

As with many other sites, you can advertise on Facebook with clickable ads that display text and graphics. You can see an example ad in Figure 7-2 (with the text "Speed up your PC"). Ads like this one can appear in a page, or so-called *social ads* can appear embedded in someone's News Feed (where they get a lot more attention). If Facebook is able to match your social ad's keywords with what's going on in someone's News Feed, it'll display your ad right in the News Feed (along with news items about the user's friends).

Starting an ad is simple, and Facebook is pushing them, so you can find links to the process all over the place. The most prominent such link is the Advertising link at the bottom of every logged-in Facebook page (that is, every Facebook page that you browse after you've logged in). Clicking that link displays the page you see shown in Figure 7-17.

This is the Facebook Ads page (http://www.facebook.com/ads/) you see in Figure 7-17, and it pushes social ads and Facebook pages. To create a new ad, click either the Get Started button or the Create Social Ad link at the bottom of the page

Figure 7-17   The Facebook Ads page

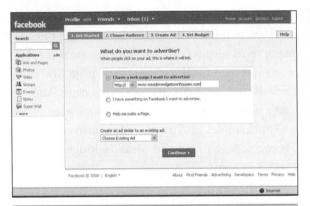

Figure 7-18   Getting started

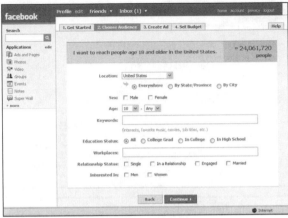

Figure 7-19   Choosing an audience

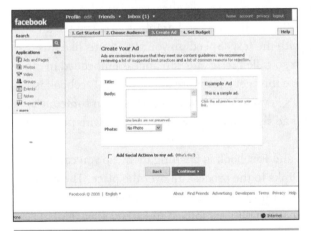

Figure 7-20   Creating the ad

(not visible in Figure 7-17)—which takes you to the page shown in Figure 7-18.

If you're advertising a landing page, enter the URL and click Continue, bringing up the page you see in Figure 7-19.

Fill in the information requested in the second page, and click Continue, bringing up the third page, as shown in Figure 7-20.

Enter the text and upload images in this page, and then click Continue, bringing up the budget page you see in Figure 7-21. Fill in your price information.

Review your ad and your payment information in the next page, and click Place Order to start your ad.

Creating an ad like this adds an Ad link to your left navigation menu of links (or an Ads And Pages link if you already have Facebook pages). Clicking that link opens your ad campaign's summary, which you can see in Figure 7-22 for a sample ad for Meadow Ridge Townhouses.

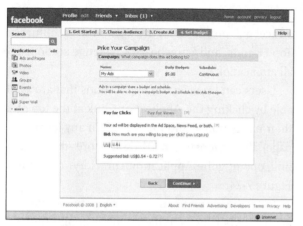

Figure 7-21   Setting the budget

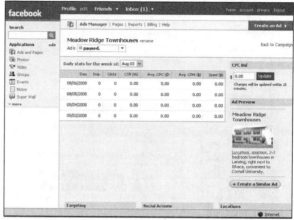

Figure 7-22   Monitoring an ad

Here, you can see all the standard data that you saw on Yahoo or Google—the number of clicks you've received, the number of views, the click-through ratio, and so on. You can also pause your campaign by selecting Paused from the drop-down list at top. And note that if Facebook thinks you're not spending enough on your ad, you'll see a red-and-pink box urging you to spend more on this page.

One of the good things about Facebook ads is that you can target specific demographics by age, gender, location, and so on, and that can be great—but if you are looking for people over the age of 30, they're few and far between on Facebook.

Using Facebook Applications

One of the most popular aspects of Facebook—and one of the best for marketers—is Facebook *applications*. Applications are embeddable into users' profile pages and run there in their own section. For example, you could have an application that lets you display your favorite videos or music, play games, draw on people's pages, and so on. Some companies have commissioned their own games, which became very popular, spreading the word about those companies in a dynamic way.

Figure 7-23   Facebook applications

Figure 7-24   Browsing applications

You can see a few representative applications in a Facebook profile in Figure 7-23—the FaceBlurb, Top Friends, and Snowboard Challenge sections are all applications.

Users can browser the applications that are available by clicking the Applications link at the top of their navigation menu (on the left in any logged-in page), then choosing the Browse More Applications link, opening the Application Directory you see in Figure 7-24.

Click the name of any application to see the application's page, and then add the application to your profile with the Add Application link in that page.

Unless you're a programmer, I don't recommend creating your application from scratch. I've discussed the process and created Facebook applications in other books, and it takes some effort. On the other hand, one of the ways that application developers make money is to allow their applications to display ads, and here are a few ad networks that will let you advertise in many Facebook applications:

- **AdBrite**   www.adbrite.com/mb/howitworks.php

- **SocialMedia**   www.socialmedia.com

- **RockYou**   www.rockyou.com

- **Adonomics**   www.adonomics.com

- **Lookery**   www.lookery.com

If nothing will do but creating your own Facebook application, other companies will develop Facebook applications for you from scratch—and usually, prices are quite reasonable:

- **Art & Logic**   www.artlogic.com

- **Notice Technologies**   www.noticetechnologies.com

- **Ayoka**   www.ayokasystems.com

- **Invoke**   www.invokemedia.com/facebook-and-social-network-application-developers/

- **Emerge**   http://emergedgtl.com/widgets

- **Parnassus Group**   http://parnassusgroup.com/category/facebook-services/

Note, however, that tens of thousands of Facebook applications are out there, all jostling for space. To get an appreciable number of users, yours has to be something special. But if yours is a hit, there's nothing like it as far as marketing on Facebook goes.

And that's it for our overview of Facebook marketing. As I said at the beginning of the chapter, we don't have the space here to go into great depth—and we haven't even touched on some topics like Facebook Events (tied to a specific date and place you can rally people around), Facebook Beacon (a controversial program to let you track your friends' actions in your News Feed on sites that are off Facebook, such as Amazon or other commercial sites—including yours), and the Facebook Marketplace (something like craigslist for Facebook users).

Server-side Power: PHP

So far, we haven't dealt a lot with working on the server, but that's about to change. In this chapter and the next, we'll take a look at working with PHP—a web-based programming language—on the server. Most ISPs now offer support for PHP, and you can do very powerful things with it. You can save data in files (such as guestbooks) on the server; interact with SQL databases; accept and read user input in HTML controls like text fields, check boxes, and so on; set and read cookies; even draw graphics on the server (such as an interactive stock chart) and send them back to the browser. We'll see all these topics in this and the next chapter.

In this first chapter on PHP, we'll get started with the topic and emphasize the use of HTML controls, letting you read the data the user enters via text fields, option buttons, and so on. Using controls to gather and respond to user input is a big part of business web sites, and we'll see how to work with them here.

Your First PHP Script

I'm going to assume that you have an ISP that can run PHP files, and that you can upload PHP files to that ISP, or that you've set up QuickPHP to test self-contained PHP files. On some ISPs' servers, especially UNIX-based servers, you have to give your PHP scripts executable permission (as well as readable permission) before they can be executed. On such servers, a permission setting of 755 will do well to allow your scripts to run. If you have a UNIX-based server and don't know about file permissions, ask your ISP's tech staff for the details.

Here's a first PHP script, first.php (PHP scripts have the extension .php). It runs a function that comes with PHP—`phpinfo`—which gives you some details about your PHP installation:

```
<?php
   phpinfo();
?>
```

You can see the results in Figure 8-1, where PHP is telling us all about itself.

Notice what's happening here—the call to the PHP function `phpinfo` is enclosed in the markup `<?php` and `?>`. That markup is there so the server can tell the difference between code it's supposed to execute as PHP and as HTML, because you can use HTML in your scripts—as long as you surround your PHP with `<?php` and `?>`. Here's an example, second.php:

PHP Version 5.2.0

System	Windows NT DM8400 5.1 build 2600
Build Date	Nov 2 2006 11:50:55
Configure Command	cscript /nologo configure.js "--enable-snapshot-build" "--with-gd=shared"
Server API	CGI/FastCGI
Virtual Directory Support	enabled
Configuration File (php.ini) Path	C:\Program Files\PHP\php.ini
PHP API	20041225
PHP Extension	20060613
Zend Extension	220060519
Debug Build	no
Thread Safety	enabled
Zend Memory Manager	enabled
IPv6 Support	enabled
Registered PHP Streams	php, file, data, http, ftp, compress.zlib
Registered Stream Socket Transports	tcp, udp

Figure 8-1 A first PHP script

MEMO

Of course, PHP is a huge topic. My goal is give you a good working knowledge of the subject in this and the next chapter—enough to use PHP with business web sites—but there's obviously more PHP than we can cover here. If you're interested, check out a good book on PHP. We're not going to have space to cover many advanced features, especially object-oriented PHP, here.

MEMO

If you're using WordPad in Windows XP to save your PHP scripts, note that WordPad doesn't understand the extension .php, so it'll give your files the extension .php.txt. The way around that is to surround the name of the file you're saving in quotation marks, "first.php", when you save the file. That'll save first.php, not first.php.txt.

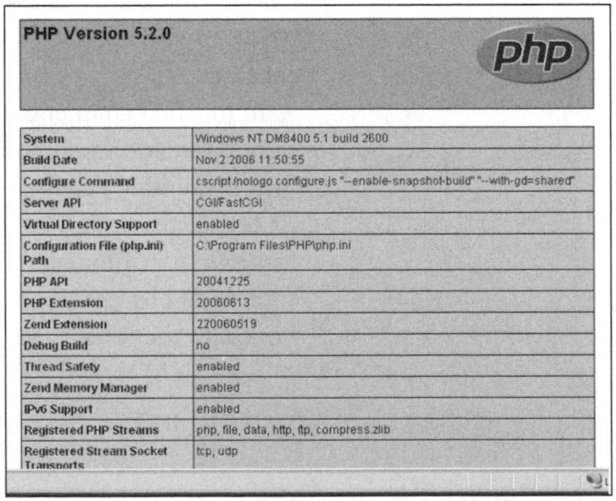

```
<html>
    <head>
        <title>
            Mixing HTML and PHP!
        </title>
    </head>

    <body>
        <h1>
            Mixing HTML and PHP!
        </h1>
        <?php
            phpinfo();
        ?>
    </body>
</html>
```

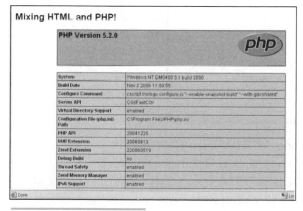

You can see second.php at work in Figure 8-2, where the HTML we've put in also shows up.

187

Displaying Text

Okay, that's a fine start. Now how about displaying some text of our own? You can do that with the PHP `echo` function, as in this example, messages.php (parentheses in function calls are optional in PHP):

Figure 8-2 A second PHP script

```
<html>
    <head>
        <title>
            Using the echo statement
        </title>
    </head>

    <body>
        <h1>
            Echoing some text:
```

```
              </h1>
              <?php
                  echo "Hello from PHP.";
              ?>
              <h1>
                  Echoing some more text:
              </h1>
              <?php
                  echo "Hello from PHP again!";
              ?>
          </body>
</html>
```

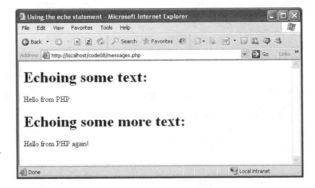

Figure 8-3   Echoing text using PHP

The results of messages.php appear in Figure 8-3.

Besides using it with plain text, you can use the `echo` function to send HTML to the browser (just echo your HTML like text), giving you the capability of writing your web pages interactively on the server.

Handling Variables

Like any other computer language, PHP can use variables—and, as with JavaScript, you don't need to formally declare variables before you use them (as you do in many languages, such as Java). In PHP, variables begin with a dollar sign ($). Here's an example, variables.php, that assigns values to a variable named `$apples`. You can pass multiple items to the `echo` function to send back to the browser if you separate them with commas.

```
<html>
    <head>
        <title>
            Assigning values to variables
        </title>
    </head>
    <body>
        <h1>
            Assigning values to variables
        </h1>
        <?php
            echo "Setting number of apples to 1.<br>";

            $apples = 1;

            echo "Number of apples: ", $apples, "<br>";

            echo "Adding 3 more apples.<br>";

            $apples = $apples + 3;

            echo "Number of apples now: ", $apples, "<br>";
        ?>
    </body>
</html>
```

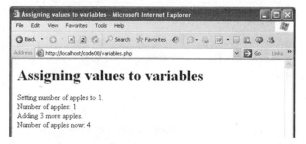

Figure 8-4   Using variables in PHP

The result appears in Figure 8-4.

Note that we used two PHP operators in this example—the assignment operator, =, and the addition operator, +. Those are only two of the PHP operators.

Using PHP Operators

PHP comes with lots of built-in operators to let you work on data, such as the addition operator +, the subtraction operator −, and so on. Here's an example using some PHP operators, operators.php. This example includes the modulus operator, %, which returns the remainder after dividing two numbers.

```html
<html>
    <body>
        <h1>Some PHP operators</h1>
        <?php
            echo "5 + 2 = ", 5 + 2, "<br>";
            echo "5 - 2 = ", 5 - 2, "<br>";
            echo "5 * 2 = ", 5 * 2, "<br>";
            echo "5 / 2 = ", 5 / 2, "<br>";
            echo "5 % 2 = ", 5 % 2, "<br>";
        ?>
    </body>
</html>
```

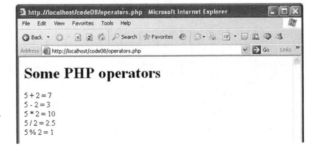

Figure 8-5   Using operators in PHP

You can see the results in Figure 8-5.

Most of the operators in PHP are the same as in JavaScript, so you already know them. You can see the PHP operators in Table 8-1; they're arranged in order of precedence. An operator with higher precedence will be executed before one of lower precedence, even if they're in the same statement, so 2 + 4 / 2 is 4, not 3—if you want to do the addition first, use parentheses like this: (2 + 4) / 2, which is 3.

```
new
[
! ~ ++ -- (int) (float) (string) (array) (object)
@
* / %
+ - .
<< >>
< <= > >=
== != === !==
&
^
|
&&
||
? :
= += -= *= /= .= %= &= |= ^= <<= >>=,
print
and
xor
or
,
```

Table 8-1   PHP Operators, in Order of Precedence

Making Choices with if Statements

Like JavaScript, PHP has an if statement, and it works the same way. Here's an example, if.php, that checks the value in a variable named $minutes:

```html
<html>
    <head>
        <title>Using the if statement</title>
    </head>
```

```
<body>
    <h1>Using the if statement</h1>
    <?php
        $minutes= 4;
        if($minutes > 3) {
            echo "Your time is up!<br>";
            echo "Please put the phone down.";
            $hang_up_now = true;
        }
    ?>
</body>
</html>
```

You can see the results in Figure 8-6.

Figure 8-6   Using the if statement in PHP

Like JavaScript, PHP also has an else statement that you use with if statements. As a bonus, it also has an elseif statement that is a mix of if and else. It lets you check a condition and execute code, allowing you to make decision "ladders" in your code like this, in my example file named elseif.php:

```
<?php
    $test_score = 78;

    if ($test_score > 90) {
        echo "You got an A!";
    }
    elseif ($test_score > 80) {
        echo "You got a B.";
    }
    elseif ($test_score > 70) {
        echo "You got a C.";
    }
    elseif ($test_score > 60) {
        echo "You got a D.";
    }
```

```
    else {
        echo "Uh oh.";
    }
?>
```

You can see the results in Figure 8-7.

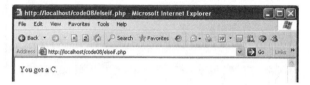

Figure 8-7   Using the
elseif statement in PHP

Using PHP for Loops

Also as in JavaScript, PHP supports a for loop. The syntax is just the same as in JavaScript, and here's an example, for.php:

```
<html>
    <head>
        <title>
            Using the for loop
        </title>
    </head>

    <body>
        <h1>
            Using the for loop
        </h1>
        <?php
            for ($loop_counter = 0; $loop_counter < 6;
                $loop_counter++){
                    echo "I'm going to display this six times.<br>";
            }
        ?>
    </body>
</html>
```

The results appear in Figure 8-8.

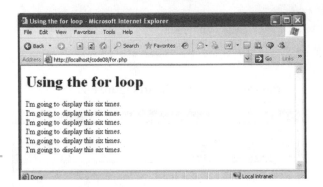

Figure 8-8   Using the `for` loop in PHP

Arrays and foreach Loops

Here's some more PHP technology—arrays. Arrays in PHP are much like those in JavaScript: they can contain strings, numbers, or objects. And, as in JavaScript, you create them with the `array` function like this:

```
$arr = array("apples", "oranges", "bananas");
```

This creates the array `$arr`, where `$arr[0]` is `"apples"`, `$arr[1]` is `"oranges"`, and `$arr[2]` is `"bananas"`. There's a special loop built into PHP that you can use to loop over arrays (in addition to the `for` loop, of course)—the `foreach` loop. This loop is useful because it automatically loops over the entire array—you don't have to make sure you set up the loop index in a `for` loop to catch all array elements. To use this loop, you enclose an expression like `$arr as $value` in parentheses, meaning that each time through the loop, that variable you've named `$value` will be assigned the next element from the `$arr` array. Here's what that looks like in array.php (note that we're also using another PHP trick here—placing a variable like `$value` inside double quotation marks will make PHP insert the value in `$value` into the string's text at that point, a process called *interpolation*):

```
<html>
    <head>
        <title>
            Using the foreach loop
```

```
                    </title>
                </head>

                <body>
                    <h1>Using the foreach loop</h1>

                        <?php
                            $arr = array("apples", "oranges", "bananas");
                            foreach ($arr as $value) {
                                echo "The fruit: $value<br>";
                            }
                        ?>
                </body>
            </html>
```

And the results, where the `foreach` loop has looped over all the elements in the `$arr` array, appear in Figure 8-9.

Figure 8-9   Using arrays in PHP

Here's another array example, modify.php. It shows how to modify an array, which also shows that, in PHP, if you reference an array name with an empty pair of square brackets after it, PHP will add another element to the end of the array automatically (allowing you to append data to arrays). Note also the `count` function, which returns the length of an array:

```
<html>
    <head>
        <title>
            Modifying an array
        </title>
    </head>

    <body>
        <h1>
            Modifying an array
        </h1>

        <?php
```

```
                              $fruits[0] = "pineapple";
                              $fruits[1] = "pomegranate";
                              $fruits[2] = "tangerine";

                              $fruits[2] = "watermelon";

                              $fruits[] = "grapes";

                              for ($index = 0; $index < count($fruits); $index++){
                                  echo $fruits[$index], "<br>";                    }
                          ?>
                     </body>
                 </html>
```

Figure 8-10   Modifying an array

The results appear in Figure 8-10.

Here's one thing more about arrays in PHP—you can use words, not just numbers, as the array index. For example, $data["hamburgers"] = 3 stores a value of 3 in $data["hamburgers"]. You can also use two-dimensional arrays in PHP, like this: $arr[4][3], which refers to the element in the $arr array in row 4, column 3.

Reading Data from HTML Controls

With all that PHP under our belts, it's time to get to the real meat of this chapter from a business site developer's point of view—interpreting the data the user has entered into HTML controls before clicking the Submit button. It's hard to think of many business web sites without thinking of HTML controls, such as text fields, check boxes, option buttons, and so on, and now we'll see how you extract the data from those controls and make use of it in your own business sites.

HTML controls like option buttons appear in HTML <form> elements, and we'll configure those <form> elements so the data in their controls is sent to our PHP scripts, by using these <form> attributes:

■ **action**   This attribute gives the URL of the PHP script that will handle the form data. You can omit this attribute, in which case its default is the URL of the current document.

■ **method**   Specifies the HTTP method or protocol for sending data to the target action URL. Common values are GET or POST.

■ **target**   Indicates a named frame for the browser to display the form results in.

Okay, let's jump into this topic by exploring text fields.

Reading Data from Text Fields

Here's an example, text.html, that displays a text field and asks the users their name. When the users click the Submit button, the browser will send the data the users have typed into the URL phptext.php (as set by the `<form>` element's `action` attribute):

```
<html>
    <head>
        <title>
            Using text fields
        </title>
    </head>

    <body>
        <center>

            <h1>
                Using text fields
            </h1>

            <form method="post" action="phptext.php">
                What's your name?

                <input name="name" type="text">

                <br>
```

```
                    <br>

                    <input type="submit" value="Submit">
                </form>

            </center>
        </body>
    </html>
```

You can see text.html at work in Figure 8-11, where I'm entering some text into the text field.

Figure 8-11   Entering data into a text field

Now what about phptext.php, which is supposed to read the text the user entered into the text field? The text field in text.html is given the name "*name*" (that is, it holds the user's name), so we have to be able to read the text from the text field named "*name*" in phptext.php. It turns out that data sent to a PHP script using the HTTP POST method is available in a PHP array named $_POST, data sent with the GET method is available to you in PHP scripts as $_GET, and the $_REQUEST array holds data that is sent with either GET or POST. So we can read the data sent to us from the text field with the expression $_REQUEST["name"] like this in phptext.php:

```
<html>
    <head>
        <title>
            Using text fields
        </title>
    </head>

    <body>
        <center>

            <h1>
                Reading data from text fields
```

```
            </h1>
            Your name is
            <?php
                echo $_REQUEST["name"];
            ?>
        </center>
    </body>
</html>
```

Figure 8-12   Reading data from a text field

Great—but does it work? Yes, it does, as you can see in Figure 8-12, where we're reading the text the user entered into the text field. Cool!

Note that to make this example work, you should store phptext.php in the same directory as text.html so the browser can find the PHP script. If you store phptext.php somewhere else, make sure you include its URL like this:

```
<form method="post"
action="http://www.terrificgreatisp.com/steve/phptext.php">
```

Reading Data from Text Areas

Text fields just give you one line of text—but you can have unlimited lines with text areas. Here's an example, textarea.html:

```
<html>
    <head>
        <title>Using text areas</title>
    </head>

    <body>
        <center>
        <h1>Using text areas</h1>
            <form method=post action="phptextarea.php">
                Please list your best friends:
                <br>
                <textarea name="friends" cols="50" rows="5">
```

```
                          1.
                          2.
                          3.
                          4.
                                    </textarea>
                                    <br>
                                    <br>
                                    <input type="submit">
                                </form>
                          </center>
                     <body>
                </html>
```

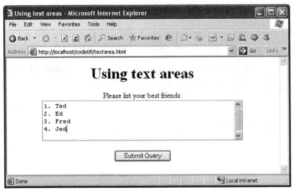

You can see textarea.html in Figure 8-13, where I'm entering some names. Now we can create the PHP script the data is sent to, phptextarea.php (as indicated by the `action` attribute in textarea .html). Once again, we can retrieve the text using the `$_REQUEST` array, this time using the name of the text area, `friends`, as the index into the array in phptextarea.php:

Figure 8-13   Entering data into a text area

```
<html>
    <head>
        <title>
            Using text areas
        </title>
    </head>

    <body>
        <center>
            <h1>
                Retrieving data from text areas
            </h1>

            Your best friends are:
            <?php
```

```
                                echo $_request["friends"];
                    ?>

                    </center>
                </body>
            </html>
```

Retrieving data from text areas

Your best friends are: 1. Ted 2. Ed 3. Fred 4. Jed

Figure 8-14   Reading data from a text area

You can see the results in Figure 8-14, where phptextarea.php was successful in reading the text from the text area.

Reading Data from Check Boxes

How do you detect whether a check box has been checked? Here's an example, checkbox.html, that asks users if they want cash back—note that the check boxes are named "check1" and "check2" and have the values "yes" and "no":

```
<html>
    <head>
        <title>Using checkboxes</title>
    </head>

    <body>
        <center>
        <h1>Using checkboxes</h1>
        <form method=post action="phpcheckbox.php">
            Do you want cash back?
            <input name="check1" type="checkbox" value="yes">
            yes
            <input name="check2" type="checkbox" value="no">
            no
            <br>
            <br>
            <input type="submit" value="Submit">
        </form>
        </center>
    </body>
</html>
```

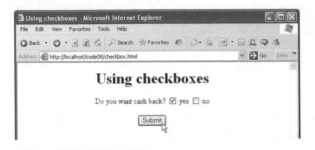

Figure 8-15   Entering data into check boxes

You can see results for checkbox.html in Figure 8-15.

But now in the PHP script that reads the check boxes, phpcheckbox.php, we have a dilemma. We can't just display $_REQUEST["check1"], because if that check box isn't checked, $_REQUEST["check1"] is undefined, and it will display "undefined" in the web page. So we have to see if $_REQUEST["check1"] is defined first, and we can do that with the isset function. If a check box's element in $_REQUEST is defined, that check box was checked, and that element will equal the value assigned to the check box (that's "yes" or "no" here). So here's how we check on the check boxes in phpcheckbox.php:

```html
<html>
    <head>
        <title>
            Using checkboxes
        </title>
    </head>

    <body>
        <center>
            <h1>Retrieving data from checkboxes</h1>
            You checked
            <?php
                if (isset($_REQUEST["check1"]))
                    echo $_REQUEST["check1"], "<br>";
                if (isset($_REQUEST["check2"]))
                    echo $_REQUEST["check2"], "<br>";
            ?>
        </center>
    </body>
</html>
```

You can see the results in Figure 8-16. Very cool.

202

Figure 8-16   Reading data from check boxes

Reading Data from Radio Buttons

Actually, the previous example ("Do you want cash back?") would be better implemented with radio buttons, because the answers are mutually exclusive ("yes" and "no"). Here's the same example using radio buttons, radio.html—note that the radio buttons are both named `"radio1"` (which puts them into the same radio button group—when one is clicked, the other one will unclick itself), and their values are `"yes"` and `"no"`:

```
<html>
    <head>
        <title>Using radio buttons</title>
    </head>
    <body>
        <center>
            <h1>Using radio buttons</h1>
            <form method="post" action="phpradio.php">
                Would you like cash back?
                <input name="radio1" type="radio" value="yes">
                yes
                <input name="radio1" type="radio" value="no">
                no
                <br>
                <br>
                <input type="submit" value="submit">
            </form>
        </center>
    </body>
</html>
```

You can see the results of radio.html in Figure 8-17.
And here's phpradio.php, where we determine which radio button was selected:

```
<html>
    <head>
```

Figure 8-17   Reading data from radio buttons

Figure 8-18   Reading data from radio buttons

```
            <title>Using radio buttons</title>
    </head>
    <body>
        <center>
            <h1>Retrieving data from radio buttons</h1>
            <?php
                echo "You selected ", $_REQUEST["radio1"];
            ?>
        </center>
    </body>
</html>
```

And phpradio.php appears at work in Figure 8-18.

Reading Data from List Boxes

Another popular HTML control is list boxes, which let the user make multiple selections. Here's an example showing how to use them, list.html, which lets the user select various fruits. This is a multiple-selection list box, as indicated by the `multiple` stand-alone attribute in the list box's `<select>` element.

```
<html>
    <head>
        <title>Using lists</title>
    </head>

    <body>
        <center>
```

```
                     <h1>Using lists</h1>
                     <form method="post" action="phplist.php">
                         Select your favorite fruit(s):
                         <br>
                         <br>
                         <select name="food[]" multiple>
                             <option>apple</option>
                             <option>orange</option>
                             <option>pear</option>
                             <option>pomegranate</option>
                         </select>
                         <br>
                         <br>
                         <input type="submit" value="Submit">
                     </form>
                 </center>
             </body>
     </html>
```

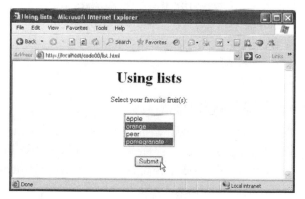

You can see the list. html results in Figure 8-19, where I'm selecting two fruits. (Hold down the CTRL key in Windows to select multiple items with the mouse.)

For a multiple-selection list box, $_REQUEST itself holds an array of all the items the user clicked. You can use a foreach loop over that array to display all the selected items in phplist.php:

Figure 8-19 Entering data into a list box

```
<html>
    <head>
        <title>Using lists</title>
    </head>
```

```
<body>
    <center>
        <h1>Retrieving data from lists</h1>
        You selected:
        <br>
        <?php
        foreach($_REQUEST["food"] as $fruit){
            echo $fruit, "<br>";
        }
        ?>
    </center>
</body>
</html>
```

You see the results in Figure 8-20, where the items the user selected are displayed. Very nice!

Figure 8-20   Reading data from list boxes

Uploading Files

The last HTML control we'll take a look at is the file upload control, which lets the user upload files. Here's what it looks like in an example, file.html. To make this work, you have to set the <form> element's enctype attribute to "multipart/form-data":

```
<html>
    <head>
        <title>
            Uploading files
        </title>
    </head>

    <body>
```

```
<center>
    <h1>
        Uploading files
    </h1>

    <form
        enctype="multipart/form-data"
        action="phpfile.php" method="post">
        Upload this file: <input name="userfile"

        type="file" />
        <br>
        <br>
        <input type="submit" value="Upload file" />
    </form>
</center>
</body>
</html>
```

Figure 8-21   Uploading a file

You can see file.html in Figure 8-21, where I've browsed to a file named data.txt, which has these contents:

```
Here is the file's data.
```

The name we've given to the file control is `"userfile"`, and you can refer to the temporary name given to the file on the server as `$_FILES['userfile']['tmp_name']`. We'll take a look at file handling in PHP in the next chapter, but here's a preview—you use the `fopen` function to open the file, giving you a *file handle,* which stands for the file as far as PHP goes. You can loop over the file, reading its contents, with a `while` loop, which keeps looping while its condition is true. For the condition, you use the expression `!feof($handle)` ("feof" stands for "file end-of-file") that is true until we reach the end of the file. Then it becomes false, ending the `while` loop. You read strings from the file using the `fgets` function, and when you're done with the file, you close it with the `fclose` function. Here's what it looks like in phpfile.php:

```html
<html>
    <head>
        <title>Retrieving file data</title>
    </head>
    <body>
        <center>
            <h1>Retrieving file data</h1>
            <br>
            Here are the contents of the file:
            <br>
            <?php
                $handle = fopen($_FILES['userfile']


                    ['tmp_name'], "r");
                while (!feof($handle)){
                    $text = fgets($handle);
                    echo $text, "<br>";
                }
                fclose($handle);
            ?>
        </center>
    </body>
</html>
```

You can see the results in Figure 8-22, where, indeed, the example uploaded data.txt and displayed its contents. Terrific.

Figure 8-22   Reading a file on the server

Creating PHP Functions

As the last topic in this chapter, we'll take a look at working with functions in PHP. That's easy, because the basic syntax for PHP functions is the same as that for JavaScript functions. Here's an example, function.php, that checks the temperature in a function named check_temperature, which returns a value of TRUE or FALSE, which is then used in an if statement:

```
<html>
    <head>
        <title>Using functions in PHP</title>
    </head>

    <body>
        <h1>Using functions in PHP</h1>

        <?php
            $degrees = 67;

            if(check_temperature($degrees)){
                echo "Nice day.";
            }
            else {
                echo "Not so nice day.";
            }

            function check_temperature($temperature)
            {
                if($temperature > 65 && $temperature < 75){
                    return TRUE;
                }
                return FALSE;
            }
        ?>
    </body>
</html>
```

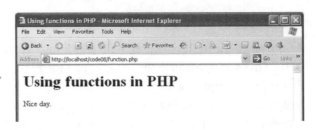

Figure 8-23   Passing data to and returning data from functions

You can see the results of function.php in Figure 8-23.

That's it for this chapter, where we got a solid start in PHP. In the next chapter, we're going to push the PHP envelope.

PHP: Cookies, Sessions, Browsers, and More

In this chapter, we're going to turn PHP loose and push the envelope. Cookies, sessions, drawing images on the server, determining the browser type, and more—it's all here. Let's dig in at once with cookies.

Cookies

We saw in Chapter 3 how JavaScript lets you set and read cookies, and you can do the same thing in PHP. To set a cookie, just use the PHP function `setCookie`, passing it the name of the cookie and the text you want to store in the cookie, as in setcookie.php, which sets a cookie named `message` to the text "`No worries.`":

```php
<?php
    setcookie("message", "No worries.");
?>

<html>
    <head>
        <title>
            Setting a cookie
        </title>
    </head>

    <body>
        <center>
            <h1>
                Setting a cookie
            </h1>
            Cookie has been set! Look at
                <a href="getcookie.php">phpgetcookie.php</a> next.
        </center>
    <body>
</html>
```

You can see setcookie.php at work in Figure 9-1. There's a link in Figure 9-1 to the PHP script, getcookie.php, that will read the cookie. In that script, we recover the cookie by passing its name as an index into the $_COOKIE array like this:

Figure 9-1   Setting a cookie in PHP

```
<html>
    <head>
        <title>
            Getting a cookie
        </title>
    </head>

    <body>
        <center>
            <h1>Getting a cookie</h1>
            The cookie says:
            <?php
                if (isset($_COOKIE['message'])) {
                    echo $_COOKIE['message'];
                }
            ?>
        </center>
    <body>
</html>
```

Getting a cookie

The cookie says: No worries.

Figure 9-2   Getting a cookie's text

You can see the result, where getcookie.php successfully recovered the cookie's value, in Figure 9-2.

By default, cookies will be erased when the browser is closed. You can set the time (in seconds) that the cookie should last, as the third parameter passed to setCookie. The following code makes the cookie last 30 days:

```
<?php
    setCookie("message", "no worries for 30 days.",
      time()+60*60*24*30);
?>

<html>
    <head>
        <title>
            Setting a configured cookie
        </title>
    </head>

    <body>
```

```
                    <center>
                        <h1>Setting a configured cookie</h1>
                        Cookie has been set to expire in 30 days! Look at
                            <a href="getcookie.php">getcookie.php</a> next.
                    </center>
                <body>
            </html>
```

Saving Data in Sessions

One big problem in web applications is that your data is limited to the current web page. So how do you keep track of, say, the user's purchases? One way is to use cookies, but there's another, more powerful way—you can store data in *sessions* on the server.

A session lets you store data in the $_SESSION array, and that data will be saved for your web application until there has been no activity from the user for a set timeout period, which is 15 minutes by default. Here's an example, session.php, that stores the temperature in the session:

```
<html>
    <head>
        <title>
            Storing data in sessions
        </title>
    </head>

    <body>
        <center>
            <h1>
                Storing data in sessions
            </h1>

            <?php
                session_start();
                $_SESSION['temperature'] = "72";
            ?>

            Stored the temperature as 72 degrees.
```

214

```
                              <br>
                              To read the temperature in a new page,
                                    <a href="session2.php">click here</a>.
                        </center>
                  <body>
            </html>
```

You can see session.php at work in Figure 9-3.

There's a link in Figure 9-3 to session2.php, where we'll read the data we stored in the $_SESSION array under the keyword temperature. Here's what session2.php looks like:

Figure 9-3   Storing data in a session

```
<html>
      <head>
            <title>
                  Retrieving data in sessions
            </title>
      </head>

      <body>
            <center>
                  <h1>
                        Retrieving data in sessions
                  </h1>

                  <?php
                        session_start();

                        if(isset($_SESSION["temperature"])){
                          echo "Welcome. The temperature is " ,
                          $_SESSION['temperature'];


                        }
                  ?>
            </center>
      <body>
</html>
```

215

Retrieving data in sessions

Welcome. The temperature is 72

Figure 9-4   Reading data
from a session

You can see the results in Figure 9-4, where we've successfully recovered the data we'd stored in the session. Very cool!

Sessions are very powerful and have the ability to make your web applications into desktop applications—in terms of data, anyway. Each session is user specific, so you'll be storing the data only from the current user that you're dealing with in your code (no matter how many people are on your site at the same time).

Determining Browser Type

Different browsers have different capabilities, and you might want to determine what type of browser the user has. We saw how to do this in JavaScript in Chapter 3, but you can also do it in PHP. Here's an example, browser.html and browser.php, that checks if the user is using Internet Explorer, and if so, displays text in an element unique to Internet Explorer—the `<marquee>` element, which makes text scroll across the screen. We start with browser.html, which has a button that, when clicked, navigates you to browser.php:

```html
<html>
    <head>
        <title>Determining browser type</title>
    </head>
    <body>
        <center>
        <h1>Determining browser type</h1>
        <form method="post" action="browser.php">
        Click the button....
        <input type="submit" value="Submit">
        </form>
        </center>
    </body>
</html>
```

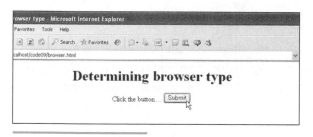

You can see browser.html in Figure 9-5.

You're dealing with Internet Explorer if the $_SERVER array's "HTTP_USER_AGENT" index returns a string that contains the text "MSIE" in it, which we can check like this in browser.php. If we're dealing with Internet Explorer, we display a <marquee> element:

Figure 9-5   Checking browser type

```html
<html>
    <head>
        <title>Determining browser type</title>
    </head>
    <body>
        <center>
            <h1>Determining browser type</h1>
            <br>
            <?php
                if(strpos($_SERVER["HTTP_USER_AGENT"], "MSIE")){
                    echo("<marquee><h1>You're using Internet
                        Explorer</h1></marquee>");
                }
                else {
                    echo("<center><h1>You are not using Internet
                        Explorer</h1></center>");
                }
            ?>
        </center>
    </body>
</html>
```

You can see the results of browser.php in Figure 9-6, where the example has recognized Internet Explorer and is displaying text in a <marquee> element.

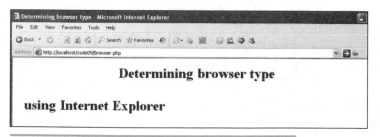

Figure 9-6   Recognizing Internet Explorer

217

Redirecting Users

You can also redirect the user to the sites you want by using PHP. Say you have three PHP scripts: script1.php, script2.php, and script3.php. Here's an example that has three forms in it and that lets the user select among these three scripts:

```html
<html>
    <head>
        <title>Redirecting the user</title>
    </head>

    <body>
        <h1>Redirecting the user</h1>

        Which script would you like to see?
        <form name="form1" action="redirect.php" method="post">
            <input type="submit" name="button" value="script1">
        </form>
        <form name="form2" action="redirect.php" method="post">
            <input type="submit" name="button" value="script2">
        </form>
        <form name="form3" action="redirect.php" method="post">
            <input type="submit" name="button" value="script3">
        </form>
        </script>
    </body>
</html>
```

The actual work is done by redirect.php. You get the name of the script to redirect the user to from the value of the button that was clicked and put together a redirection string, such as `"location: script1.php"`. Then you use that string as an HTTP header sent back to the browser—which redirects the browser to the new location you specify:

```php
<?php
    $redirect = "location: " . $_REQUEST['button'] , ".php";
    echo header($redirect);
?>
```

Creating Single-Page Scripts

So far, most of our PHP examples have needed at least two files—an HTML page and a PHP script, or two PHP scripts. However, you can wrap everything into one script as well. The way to do this is to check the $_REQUEST array to see if there's any data waiting for you. If not, display the welcome page. If there's data waiting for you, process that data.

Here's an example, text.php, that asks users their name using a text field named "name". If $_REQUEST["name"] is set when the script loads, the user's name is waiting for you to display it. If not, you should ask the user his or her name. Here's what text.php looks like:

```
<html>
    <head>
        <title>Using text fields</title>
    </head>
    <body>
        <center><h1>Using text fields</h1>
        <?php
            if(isset($_REQUEST["name"])){
        ?>
            Your name is
        <?php
            echo $_REQUEST["name"];
            }
            else {
        ?>
            <form method="post" action="text.php">
                What's your name?
                <input name="name" type="text">
                <br><br>
                <input type="submit" value="Submit">
            </form>
        <?php
            }
        ?>
        </center>
    </body>
</html>
```

219

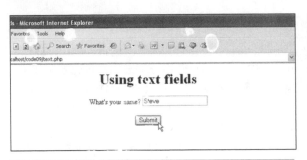

Figure 9-7   Wrapping a PHP script into a single page

Figure 9-8   Displaying the user's name

You can see text.php when you first open it in Figure 9-7, where it's asking for the user's name.

After the user enters his or her name and clicks the Submit button, the text.php script will display the user's name, as you see in Figure 9-8. Now you've wrapped two PHP scripts into a single PHP script.

This example works because it expects data to be stored under the name "name" in the $_REQUEST array. However, it might be legal in your application to leave a text field blank, which means $_REQUEST["name"] can legally be empty. In such cases, you can store text in a hidden field when the page first appears so your script can check that field and determine that the welcome page has already been displayed. An example is coming up next.

> **MEMO**
>
> Since text.php sends its data to itself, you can omit the action attribute in the <form> here. By default, if you omit the action attribute, the form's data is sent to the same script.

Performing Data Validation

Here's a more involved example showing how to perform validation on data the user has entered using PHP. This example is modeled after professional validators and stores any validation errors it finds in an array named $errors. Variables in functions are usually restricted to the function they're declared or first used in, so to let code in all the functions here access the $errors array, we declare that array as global in every function that uses it.

This example, validator.php, asks users to enter their name, and if they don't, gives them an error message and another chance to enter their name.

Here's validator.php:

```
<html>
    <head>
        <title>
            Using text fields
        </title>
    </head>

    <body>
        <center>
                <h1>Using text fields</h1>
        <?php
            $errors = array();

            if(isset($_REQUEST["seen_already"])){

                validate_data();
                if(count($errors) != 0){
                    display_errors();
                    display_welcome();
                }
                else {
                    process_data();
                }
            }
            else {
                display_welcome();
            }

            function validate_data()
            {
                global $errors;
                if($_REQUEST["name"] == "") {
                  $errors[] =
                  "<font color='red'>Please enter your name</font>";
                }
            }

            function display_errors()
            {
```

```
                                        global $errors;

                                        foreach ($errors as $err){
                                            echo $err, "<br>";
                                        }
                                    }

                                    function process_data()
                                    {
                                        echo "Your name is ";
                                        echo $_REQUEST["name"];
                                    }

                                    function display_welcome()
                                    {
                                        echo "<form method='post' action='validator.php'>";
                                        echo "What's your name?";
                                        echo "<br>";
                                        echo "<input name='name' type='text'>";
                                        echo "<br>";
                                        echo "<br>";
                                        echo "<input type='submit' value='Submit'>";
                                        echo "<input type='hidden' name='seen_already'
                                            value='hidden_data'>";
                                        echo "</form>";
                                    }
                                ?>
                                </center>
                            </body>
                        </html>
```

You can see the welcome page of validator.php in Figure 9-9.

If the users click the Submit button without entering any text, a red message (black and white in the figure) appears asking them to enter their name, as you see in Figure 9-10.

If the users then enter their name and click the button, the example shows their name, as you can see in Figure 9-11.

Figure 9-9   Requesting the user's name

Figure 9-10   Displaying a validation error

Figure 9-11   Displaying the user's name

It's easy to adapt this example to validate whatever kind of data you want—just put your code (PHP supports regular expressions, for example) in the `validate_data` function.

Removing HTML Tags

A big issue when you display user data in your web pages is embedded HTML when you display what users have added, such as in a guestbook. Nasty people can use HTML elements—even `<script>` elements—to redirect people away from your page. So you always have to check the text that users have given you before displaying it in a browser. An easy way to handle this is to use the PHP `strip_tags` function to strip the HTML tags from text, making that text safe to display in browsers. Here's how to modify the previous example to use `strip_tags`:

```
<html>
    <head><title>using text fields</title></head>
    <body>
        <center><h1>using text fields</h1>
        <?php
            .
            .
            .

            function process_data()
            {
```

```
                            echo "your name is ";
                            $ok_text = strip_tags($_request["name"]);
                            echo $ok_text;
                        }
                        .
                        .
                        .
                    ?>
                    </center></body>
            </html>
```

Preserving Data Between Accesses

When you have multiple input fields and there's a validation error, it's polite to refill the input fields the user has filled in correctly so he or she doesn't have to reenter everything due to one validation error. It's easy enough to do—you just refill the validated input fields by reading their data from the $_REQUEST array.

Here's an example, store.php, that asks for the users' first and last names. If they fill in one but not the other, the example gives them an error message—but reproduces the data in the text field that the users have already filled in so they don't have to start from scratch. Here's what store.php looks like:

```
<html>
    <head>
        <title>Preserving data</title>
     </head>

    <body>
      <center>
        <h1>Preserving data</h1>
        <?php
            $errors = array();
            if(isset($_REQUEST["seen_already"])){
                validate_data();
                if(count($errors) != 0){
```

```php
                display_errors();
                display_welcome();
        } else {
            process_data();
        }
    } else {
        display_welcome();
    }
    function validate_data()
    {
        global $errors;
        if($_REQUEST["firstname"] == "") {
            $errors[] =
                "<font color='red'>Please enter your first
                    name</font>";
        }
        if($_REQUEST["lastname"] == "") {
            $errors[] =
                "<font color='red'>Please enter your last
                    name</font>";
        }
    }
    function display_errors()
    {
        global $errors;

        foreach ($errors as $err){
            echo $err, "<br>";
        }
    }
    function process_data()
    {
        echo "Your first name is ";
        echo $_REQUEST["firstname"];
        echo "<br>Your last name is ";
        echo $_REQUEST["lastname"];
    }
    function display_welcome()
    {
        $first_name = isset($_REQUEST["firstname"]) ?
            $_REQUEST["firstname"] : "";
```

```
                                        $last_name = isset($_REQUEST["lastname"]) ?
                                            $_REQUEST["lastname"] : "";
                                    echo "<form method='post' action='store.php'>";
                                    echo "What's your first name?";
                                    echo "<input name='firstname' type='text' value='",
                                        $first_name, "'>";
                                    echo "<br>";
                                    echo "What's your last name?";
                                    echo "<input name='lastname' type='text' value='",
                                        $last_name, "'>";
                                    echo "<br>";
                                    echo "<input type=submit value=submit>";
                                    echo "<input type=hidden name='seen_already'
                                        value='hidden_data'>";
                                    echo "</form>";
                                }
                            ?>
                        </center>
                    </body>
                </html>
```

226

Figure 9-12   Preserving data between accesses

You can see how this works in Figure 9-12, where I have omitted my last name. The store.php example gives me an error message—but also reproduces my first name as entered so I don't have to start entering both names from scratch.

Reading a File

One of the big attractions of using code on the server is that you can store and manipulate data on the server. You can save customer comments, a guestbook, even customer orders. You can treat files as either text or binary (the difference is that you can work with text files in terms of strings). For example, you can use the `fgets` function to read a string from a text file. The `feof` (file end of file) function returns `true` when you're at the end of a file. You open a file for reading or writing with `fopen`, passing it the name of the file to open and an access mode. For example, `"r"` opens a file for reading, "w" for writing, "r+" for both reading and writing, "a" for appending to the end, and "a+" for appending and reading. The fopen function returns a file handle that stands for the file in PHP terms, and you pass the file handle to functions like feof or fgets. When you're done working with the file, you close the file handle with fclose. Here's how we read a text file named file .txt and display its contents:

```html
<html>
    <head>
        <title>
            Reading a file
        </title>
    </head>
    <body>
        <center>
            <h1>
                Reading a file
            </h1>
            <?php
                $handle = fopen("file.txt", "r");
                while (!feof($handle)){
                    $text = fgets($handle);
                    echo $text, "<br>";
                }
                fclose($handle);
            ?>
        </center>
    </body>
</html>
```

If file.txt contains the string "Here is the text!" and it's in the same directory as this example, readfile.php, you can see the results in Figure 9-13.

You can use the fread function to read and to treat files in terms of bytes. Here's an example, fread.php, that opens the file for binary reading (mode "rb"), then uses the filesize function to get the size of the file in bytes. It reads in that many bytes from the file by using fread,

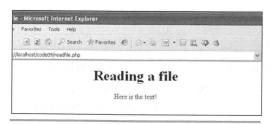

Figure 9-13   Reading a file with fgets

then replaces the end-of-line characters (the newline character, given by the string "\n") in the text with the HTML <br> element by using the PHP str_replace function. It displays the results like this:

```
<html>
    <head>
        <title>
            Reading a file with fread
        </title>
    </head>

    <body>
        <center>
            <h1>
                Reading a file with fread
            </h1>

            <?php
                $handle = fopen("file.txt", "rb");
                $text = fread($handle, filesize("file.txt"));

                $formatted_text = str_replace("\n", "<br>", $text);

                echo $formatted_text;
                fclose($handle);
            ?>

        </center>
    </body>
</html>
```

You can see the results of treating file.txt as a binary file, reading it in byte by byte, and displaying it, in Figure 9-14.

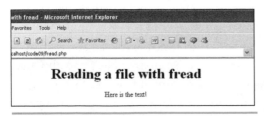

Figure 9-14   Reading a file with fread

Writing to a File

You can also store data in files on the server. PHP allows you to write in a binary way using the fwrite function— you can pass it the file handle to write to and the text to write. Here's an example, fwrite.php, that writes the text

```
Here
is
the
text!
```

to a file named text.txt. To put the words on different lines, we include the newline character, `"\n"`, in the text to write like this: `"Here\nis\nthe\ntext!"`. If `fwrite` returns `false`, it was not successful in writing the file, so we should display an error—otherwise, it wrote the file with no trouble. Here's what it looks like in fwrite.php—note that we open the file for binary writing, mode `"wb"`:

```
<html>
    <head>
        <title>
            Writing a file with fwrite
        </title>
    </head>
    <body>
        <center>
            <h1>
                Writing a file with fwrite
            </h1>

            <?php
                $handle = fopen("text.txt", "wb");

                $text = "Here\nis\nthe\ntext!";

                if (fwrite($handle, $text) == false) {
                    echo "Cannot write to text.txt.";
                }
                else {
                    echo "Created the file text.txt.";
                }
                fclose($handle);
            ?>
        </center>
    </body>
</html>
```

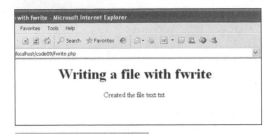

Figure 9-15 Writing a file with `fwrite`

You can see fwrite.php at work in Figure 9-15, where it's written the file text.txt.

Appending to a File

Note that when you open an existing file with mode `"w"`, it replaces the contents of that file. Sometimes, however, you want to append data to a file, and you can do that by opening a file for appending, with file mode `"a"`. Here's an example where we append some text to what's already in text.txt:

```php
<?php
$handle = fopen("text.txt", "ab");
$text = "\nAnd\nhere\nis\nmore\ntext!";
if (fwrite($handle, $text) == false) {
    echo "Cannot write to text.txt.";
}
else {
    echo "Appended to the file text.txt.";
}

fclose($handle);
?>
```

Drawing on the Server

One of the impressive things for business sites with PHP is to draw images in real time on the server. PHP has many drawing functions, which you can find online—take a look at the documentation for the PHP function we'll use here, `imageellipse`, at http://us3.php.net/imageellipse, and note the links to the dozens of drawing functions on the left.

You create an image on the server with `imagecreate`, create colors (passing R, G, and B values just as when creating HTML colors) with `imagecolorallocate`, and use functions like `imageellipse` to draw in the image. When you're done, you create an HTTP header indicating this is a JPG file, send the image to the browser with the `imagejpeg` function, and delete the image with `imagedestroy`. Here's how we draw a few ellipses against a gray background:

```php
<?php
    $image_height = 100;
    $image_width = 300;

    $image = imagecreate($image_width, $image_height);
    $back_color = imagecolorallocate($image, 200, 200, 200);
    $draw_color = imagecolorallocate($image, 0, 0, 0);
    imageellipse($image, 100, 50, 150, 50, $draw_color);
    imageellipse($image, 150, 40, 150, 50, $draw_color);
    imageellipse($image, 200, 30, 150, 50, $draw_color);
    header('content-type: image/jpeg');

    imagejpeg($image);

    imagedestroy($image);
?>
```

You can see the results of this script, draw.php, in Figure 9-16. Cool!

Drawing interactive graphics on the server is great for giving your customers real-time data, such as stock charts or performance graphs of their investments.

Note that this PHP script returns a JPG file, so if you want to embed it in an HTML page, you can use an `<img>` element like this: `<img src="draw.php">`.

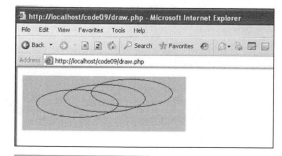

Figure 9-16   Drawing on the server

Ajax and Sending Data

One of the attractions of working with code on the server is to be able to read what you send it behind the scenes with Ajax and respond appropriately. You can send data to the server when using Ajax with either the GET or POST method. I like the POST method because it's somewhat more secure. Here's an example, poster.html, that sends a 1 or a 2 to a PHP script named dataresponder.php using a parameter named `"data"`. The dataresponder .php script reads the value of the `data` parameter and replies with a message indicating you pushed one of two buttons, button number 1 or button number 2. You indicate you want to use the `POST` method when you open the `XMLHttpRequest` object, and you send the data you want to post with the `send` method (which we passed just a null value to before). To post data, you have to use the format of URL-encoded data (without the URL). For example, to assign the value `"the text"` to a parameter named `item`, and `"more text"` to a parameter named `item2`, you would use URL-encoding like this (note the spaces become plus signs, +): `url?item=the+text&item 2=more+text`. To send our data—which is just the strings "1" or "2"—to dataresponder.php using the parameter `"data"`, we would send the string `"data=1"` or `"data=2"` to dataresponder.php. Here's what it looks like in poster.html:

```html
<html>
  <head>
    <title>Sending Data to the Server With POST</title>

    <script language = "javascript">
      var XMLHttpRequestObject = false;

      if (window.XMLHttpRequest) {
        XMLHttpRequestObject = new XMLHttpRequest();
      } else if (window.ActiveXObject) {
        XMLHttpRequestObject = new ActiveXObject(

          "Microsoft.XMLHTTP");
      }

      function getData(dataSource, divID, data)
      {
        if(XMLHttpRequestObject) {
          var obj = document.getElementById(divID);
          XMLHttpRequestObject.open("POST", dataSource);
          XMLHttpRequestObject.setRequestHeader('Content-Type',
            'application/x-www-form-urlencoded');
```

```
                    XMLHttpRequestObject.onreadystatechange = function()
                    {
                      if (XMLHttpRequestObject.readyState == 4 &&
                        XMLHttpRequestObject.status == 200) {
                          obj.innerHTML = XMLHttpRequestObject.responseText;
                      }
                    }

                    XMLHttpRequestObject.send("data=" + data);
                }
            }
        </script>
    </head>

    <body>

      <h1>Sending Data to the Server With POST</h1>

      <form>
        <input type = "button" value = "Fetch message 1"
          onclick = "getData('dataresponder.php', 'targetDiv', 1)">
        <input type = "button" value = "Fetch message 2"
          onclick = "getData('dataresponder.php', 'targetDiv', 2)">
      </form>

      <div id="targetDiv">
        <p>The fetched message will appear here.</p>
      </div>

    </body>
</html>
```

Here's the script dataresponder.php, which reads the data passed to it and indicates which button was clicked in poster.html:

```
<?php
  if ($_POST["data"] == "1") {
    echo 'You sent the server a value of 1';
  }
  if ($_POST["data"] == "2") {
    echo 'You sent the server a value of 2';
  }
?>
```

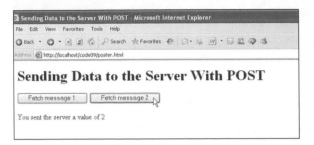

Sending Data to the Server With POST

You sent the server a value of 2

Figure 9-17   Posting data to the server using Ajax

You can see the results in Figure 9-17, where we've been able to send data to the server using Ajax behind-the-scenes methods, with no browser screen refresh needed.

Using PHP with Databases

PHP is often used to work with databases on the server, and it's particularly popular with the database software named MySQL. We don't have the space here to introduce more than a demo of PHP used with databases, but you can find all the functions you use with MySQL in PHP at http://us2.php.net/mysql_fetch_array, which is the manual page for the `mysql_fetch_array` function and lists all the MySQL functions as links on the left of the page.

This example, db.php, interacts with a database named `produce` in MySQL that has a sample table named `fruit` written for this example with these contents:

Name	Number
apples	1020
oranges	3329
bananas	8582
pears	234

The db.php script connects to MySQL with the `mysql_connect` function (you pass the database server, username, and password to this function), selects the database to work with using the `mysql_select_db` function, extracts all the table's data with the `mysql_query` function, formats the table into an array with the `mysql_fetch_array` function, displays the database table as an HTML table, and closes the database with `mysql_close`. Whew. Here's what this example, db.php, looks like:

```
<html>
  <head>
    <title>
        Displaying tables with MySQL
    </title>
  </head>

  <body>
    <h1>Displaying tables with MySQL</h1>

    <?php
      $connection = mysql_connect("localhost","username","password")
        or die ("Couldn't connect to server");

      $db = mysql_select_db("produce",$connection)
        or die ("Couldn't select database");

      $query = "SELECT * FROM fruit";
      $result = mysql_query($query)
        or die("Query failed: ".mysql_error());

      echo "<table border='1'>";
      echo "<tr>";
      echo "<th>Name</th><th>Number</th>";
      echo "</tr>";

      while ($row = mysql_fetch_array($result))
      {
        echo "<tr>";
        echo "<td>", $row['name'], "</td><td>", $row['number'],
          "</td>";
        echo "</tr>";
      }

      echo "</table>";

      mysql_close($connection);
    ?>
  </body>
</html>
```

MEMO

In fact, Joomla! uses PHP and MySQL internally. All three components— Joomla!, PHP, and MySQL—are free.

MEMO

One topic we didn't cover in this chapter is how to create an e-mail form with PHP. E-mail forms are those pages that have text fields that you can enter your message in and click a button to send e-mail. We didn't cover that because I have found PHP terribly finicky here, often demanding changes to the PHP initialization file, php. ini—which you often don't have access to on your ISP. I've written working e-mail forms in PHP, but really prefer to do this job in Perl, another online scripting language, which doesn't demand any configuration changes to send e-mail! If you want to create an e-mail form using PHP, take a look at the free code for one at www.ibdhost.com/contact/.

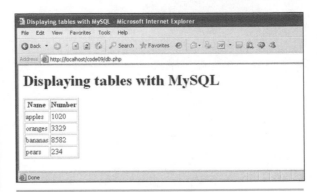

Figure 9-18   Extracting a database table using PHP

You can see the results in Figure 9-18, where we have successfully extracted the `fruit` table from MySQL in PHP.

Being able to store your data in a database is very powerful for business sites and is often how store catalogs are hosted online. If you don't have the stomach for a lot of database coding, you might check out a content management system (CMS) such as Joomla!, discussed in the next chapter. A CMS will handle the details of storing your catalog items, complete with photos, in a database and will handle formatting those items into pages when they're viewed.

And that completes our overview of PHP. As you can see, there's a lot of depth here, and there are plenty of topics we didn't have space to cover. If you're interested in more advanced material, check out one of the many books on PHP.

Taking Credit Cards Online

In this chapter, we'll take a look at the good part of online stores—getting the money. We'll learn about getting a merchant account, setting up your own shopping cart, using shopping cart software, using online store-creation software, PayPal, Google Checkout, and more.

Let's start with what's been the traditional way for merchants to start taking payments online—getting a merchant account.

Getting a Merchant Account

The traditional way to take payments online has been to get a merchant account and to use a credit-card processor, although you now have other options (such as letting your customers pay through PayPal, coming up in this chapter).

I set up my merchant account through one of the most popular gateway companies (they're a "gateway" to the credit-card processor), Authorize.Net, at www.authorize.net, shown in Figure 10-1.

They've got good customer and technical support, and you can call them at (877) 447-3938.

Figure 10-1   Authorize.Net

Here's how it works: You contact them, and they send you a "pre-application," which judges how much traffic you think you'll have. Depending on your answers, Authorize.Net will select a merchant account provider for you and then will send you two applications: one for Authorize.Net and a tougher one for the merchant account provider, to set up your merchant account.

The merchant account application will be demanding and can ask for bank statements, tax returns, social security numbers (for credit checks), and a lot more. It took me a long time to fill out and a couple of attempts before the merchant account people (Authorize.Net selected E-OnlineData for us) were satisfied.

The whole approval process took several weeks, and when you've been approved, the charges start—both companies bill your bank account monthly, and they'll charge you a percentage of your sales as well.

If your site uses shopping cart software, Authorize.Net can recommend developers it has certified to connect you to its system. You'll find a list of shopping cart software that Authorize.Net has approved at www.authorize .net/certified_solution_directory.asp?page_id=38927&type_of_solution=22673. The usual one-time cost is a few hundred dollars for this service.

As web developers, we custom-coded our site, and we don't use any standard shopping cart software. It turns out that Authoize.Net has an API (application programming interface) that specifies how to connect to Authorize.Net when a customer wants to check out. They also provide sample code in many languages, such as Perl and PHP, that uses that API to connect, and which you can modify.

We used their PHP sample code to implement our checkout. The customers click the Buy button, and that brings up the PHP file, which we modified to display a summary of their order. You customize the PHP script to pass Authorize.Net an API login ID and a transaction key, as well as the amount of the purchase. You can also set a field in the PHP script indicating that this transaction is a test, and not to actually charge the credit card.

The customers are then taken to the Authorize.Net site and asked to enter their credit card number, address, and so on. You can customize what information users should enter through a control panel that you log into with your merchant ID at Authorize.Net. The card is then charged, and a thank-you page appears on your site.

Getting all this to work, and making sure the transaction key and API login ID were entered in all the right places in the PHP script, turned out to be quite a chore and took about a week of work. We had one particular problem that no one could solve. We had a classroom site where customers could choose an instructor, and we needed to be informed after the transaction which instructor the customer had signed up with, so our automated system could e-mail notification to that instructor, and we could add the customer to the instructor's schedule. We put the instructor's ID number in a hidden field when we connected to Authorize.Net, because it passes on hidden fields that it doesn't use to the thank-you page on our site (where we would use that ID after the transaction was complete). The problem was that Firefox noticed that a web page in a secure connection (Authorize.Net) was passing data on to an unsecure connection (our site's thank-you page), and it popped a warning dialog on the screen. All the user had to do was to click OK, but it was annoying. And no one at Authorize.Net or on our team could get around it.

If you're interested in what kinds of problems come up when you do your own coding to connect to Authorize.Net, their developer FAQ is at http://developer.authorize.net/faqs/.

On the other hand, if you're not necessarily a fan of beating your head against a rock because you have a totally custom-designed site that needs customized solutions, you might want to take a look at some of the preexisting shopping-cart software out there, which is coming up next.

Using Shopping Cart Software

Dozens of shopping cart programs are available, and here's a list in no special order. All these shopping carts have been approved by Authorize.Net, which can pass you on to a certified developer who can connect your shopping cart to your account on their site. Here's the list. (Disclaimer: I haven't used any of this software and am relying on the software's online description here.)

- **CashCowCart** www.cashcowcart.com/   Search-engine friendly, e-mail marketing, traffic reporting, shipping and tax calculation, order history, quick product search and navigation, delivery notification, import/export, memberships and group discounts, related items showcase, newsletter and coupon promotions, and more.

- **ASecureCart**   https://www.asecurecart.net/main/default.aspx Supports coupons, discounts, events, and affiliate tracking. Includes inventory tracking, digital delivery, order exporting, and UPS or USPS shipping. Free 30-day trial. Free technical support.

- **Americart** www.americart.com/   Features comprehensive shipping, handling, and tax capability.

- **WebAssist** www.webassist.com/   Has a Checkout Wizard that generates the pages you'll need for the checkout process, from custom data entry to order receipt.

- **cf_ezcart ColdFusion Shopping Cart**   www.cf-ezcart.com/   Runs on ColdFusion 5.0 or higher. Discounted pricing is available with hosting, but you may host anywhere. There is a one-time license fee.

- **King Cart Services**   www.king-cart.com/   Supports real-time shipping computation including international, state/county taxes with exempt customers/products, quantity pricing, coupons, gift certificates, discounts, unlimited products, public/private pricing, currency conversion, inventory tracking, thumbnail images, download sales, searching, and affiliate program support.

- **SEO-Cart**   www.seo-cart.com/   A search engine–friendly shopping cart. Designed so that each product in your store will have a unique presence in online search engines.

- **Apple Cart**   www.spads.com/   A low-cost, high-end shopping cart that is as simple as adding a Buy button to any HTML page. You can add to the cart or go directly to check out.

- **ProductCart**   www.earlyimpact.com/   A user-friendly shopping cart written entirely in Active Server Pages (ASP).

- **Ecommerce Templates**   www.ccommercetemplates.com/   Integrates into the HTML editors such as Dreamweaver, FrontPage, and GoLive as well as CSS layouts. Gives you design and shopping cart software. Has no monthly fees and no setup charges.

- **Ecommerce Shopping Cart**   www.roicart.com/   Includes shopping cart, real-time credit-card processing, offline credit-card processing, e-mail marketing, e-mail autoresponders, coupon system, automatic shipping and tax calculation, and more. Free 30-day trial.

- **AbleCommerce**   www.ablecommerce.com/   Offers search engine–friendly software, a complete shopping cart solution available with monthly pricing or one-time license fee, asp.net 1.1/2.0, and ColdFusion and Java Server Pages (JSP).

241

- **GoldbarOne**   www.goldbar.net/   Includes shopping cart software, e-mail marketing tools, affiliate tracking, SEO optimization tools, hosting, and more.

- **SalesCart**   www.salescart.com/   Integrates with Dreamweaver and FrontPage. SalesCart supports both Linux and Windows ISP servers and open database support for Access, MSSQL, and MySQL.

- **SecureNetShop**   www.securenetshop.com/   Allows you to sell products, services, downloadable files, and eBay auction items. Supports automatic sales tax calculations, automatic shipping calculations (USPS, FedEx, and UPS), and QuickBooks compatibility. Free technical support is available seven days a week.

- **Cart Manager**   www.cartmanager.net/   Supports unlimited products and orders, customizable, real-time shipping calculations, secure checkout, eBay and QuickBooks integration, and phone and e-mail support.

- **X-Cart**   www.x-cart.com/   Features online credit-card processing, inventory tracking, order history, tax and shipping rates calculation, web-based administrator's back office, optional multivendor operation mode, and more.

- **DesignCart**   www.designcart.com/   Supports unlimited products and orders, real-time shipping calculations, simple and secure checkout, eBay and QuickBooks integration, and phone and e-mail support.

Here's a tip: When you get shopping cart software, check to see if it's "PCI/CISP compliant." PCI/CISP are standards set up by the credit card industry to ensure safe transactions, and a company like Authorize.Net insists that everyone comply with these standards.

Another popular option is to use a content management system such as Joomla! (www.joomla.org). A content management system lets you enter your content, and it'll format that content into pages for you. Joomla! has many extensions available, such as a shopping cart component that you can use to take customer orders.

You may want more than just prebuilt shopping carts, however—you may want software that builds your whole business site, from soup to nuts. That's coming up next.

Build a Store with Software

Tons of software is available that will build your entire business web site, complete with shopping cart. Here's a sampler of software and companies that provide business-site building services; all of these are approved by Authorize.Net. (Disclaimer: As before, I haven't actually used any of this software.)

- **LiveMerchant** www.bbdesign.com/ LiveMerchant software says it's "flexible, easy-to-use, and can be custom programmed to meet your needs." BB Design handles your integration and programming; no technical experience is required.

- **My Web Site Tool** www.mywebsitetool.com/en/index.php Free, live 30-day trial. Features HTML tools, import/export data, discount coupons, reward points, shipping or quantity specials, purchase order history, and much more.

- **Earth Skater Custom eCommerce** www.earthskater.net/ Provides a storefront. Offers complimentary web design and setup, saying they will guide you through the e-commerce process.

- **SCartFree SCartServer** http://shopping.scartserver.com/ Sets up through the SCart Manager online store builder. No complicated software required.

- **SightShop** www.sightworks.com/pages/services.php An online e-commerce management system that "enables non-technical people to do technical things."

- **SmartCart** www.smartcart.com/ SmartCart Enterprise is an "all-in-one ecommerce shopping cart solution and Web store builder." Features online store builder, e-commerce hosting, secure ordering system, shopping cart button maker, inventory tracking, affiliate management, digital download sales, retail and wholesale catalog access, QuickBooks integration, coupon manager, product rating and reviews, Froogle/Google feeds, and more.

- **MyCart.net** www.mycart.net/ Can work as a store that you link to from any number of outside web sites, or MyCart.net can be your entire web site. Around-the-clock technical support. Integrated UPS, FedEx, USPS, QuickBooks, and Froogle. Full-featured solution with domain registration, hosting, e-mail, shopping cart, and more.

- **Pinnacle Cart** www.pinnaclecart.com/ An e-commerce and web site builder application that allows you to customize, manage, and market your store. Supports digital products, wholesaler pricing, product data feeds to multiple sites, QuickBooks integration, Google site maps, one-page checkout, multi-currency and -language support, bulk product loader, SEO support, and more.

- **Quick Cart** www.quickcart.com/ Quick Cart Shopping Cart Store Builder is a hosted shopping cart and e-commerce store builder. No transaction fees. No setup fees.

- **VirtualStore 2000** www.vs2000.net/ Creates turnkey business sites. Can add items, pages, and categories along with graphics via a web browser. No programming experience required.

- **Interspire Shopping Cart** www.interspire.com/shoppingcart/ Combines customizable store designs with marketing tools such as e-mail marketing, coupon codes, gift certificates, and Google AdWords.

- **StoreFront** www.storefront.net/ Provides storefront building services.

- **ShopFactory**   www.shopfactory.com/   A web shop builder featuring a WYSIWYG editor with an Access database, customization functions, fraud protection, and e-commerce functions.

- **MightyMerchant**   www.mightymerchant.com/   Company that designs custom e-commerce web sites from simple to sophisticated. Designers create your custom design and can implement complex pricing and unique product displays.

- **EasyStoreCreator**   www.easystorecreator.com/   Do-it-yourself online web store builder / shopping cart. Real-time shipping rates from USPS, UPS, FedEx, and DHL. Inventory control and marketing features such as coupons, special pricing, and so on.

- **5th Avenue Shoppe**   www.5th-avenue-software.com/   Shopping cart software and storefront builder. Written in PHP utilizing MySQL database, it features wizard-based setup, web-based merchant control panel, multiple types of product options, unlimited categories and levels, powerful search and listing functions, and much more. No PHP programming or MySQL knowledge required.

- **Virtualshop**   www.virtualshop.co.uk/   Windows package for creating online shopping web sites.

- **Decentrix Website Solution**   www.decentrix.com/   Company that builds business web sites for you. Features include site visitor tracking, customer conversion metrics, and accounting reporting.

Cashing Out with PayPal

PayPal offers a quick, easy way for you to accept credit card payments online—no merchant account needed. You can start taking credit cards with their Standard package, which has the reasonable fees of $0.30 plus 1.9–2.9 percent per transaction.

PayPal appears in Figure 10-2—to learn more about taking credit cards,

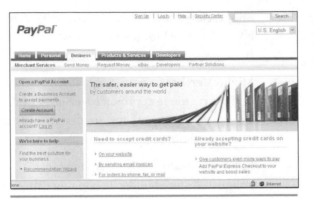

Figure 10-2   PayPal

click a link under the heading "Need to accept credit cards?"

PayPal can take payments if your customer has a PayPal account, of course, but your customers can also check out simply if they have Visa, Discover, Master-Card, American Express, or even just a bank account.

When you have a PayPal account, you can log in and click the Merchant Services tab, as shown in Figure 10-3.

Figure 10-3   Merchant Services in PayPal

For example, PayPal can create the HTML you need to display a Buy Now button. Click that option shown in Figure 10-3, opening up the customization page you see in Figure 10-4.

Fill out the required information, and Pay-Pal will display the HTML you paste into your site where you want your Buy Now button to go. Here's an example:

```
<form action="https://www.paypal.com/cgi-bin/webscr" method="post">
<input type="hidden" name="cmd" value="_xclick">
<input type="hidden" name="business" value="xxxxxx">
<input type="hidden" name="item_name" value="xxxxxx">
<input type="hidden" name="amount" value="xxxxxx">
<input type="hidden" name="shipping" value="0.00">
```

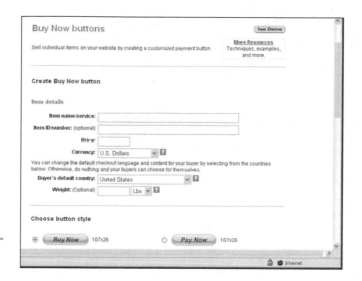

Figure 10-4   Creating a Buy
Now button

```
<input type="hidden" name="no_shipping" value="1">
<input type="hidden" name="return"
value="http://www.xxxxxxxx.com/checkout.html">
<input type="hidden" name="no_note" value="1">
<input type="hidden" name="currency_code" value="USD">
<input type="hidden" name="lc" value="US">
<input type="hidden" name="bn" value="PP-BuyNowBF">
<input type="image"
src="https://www.paypal.com/en_US/i/btn/btn_buynowCC_LG.gif"
border="0" name="submit" alt="PayPal - The safer, easier way to pay
online!">
<img alt="" border="0"
src="https://www.paypal.com/en_US/i/scr/pixel.gif" width="1"
height="1">
</form>
```

You can see such a button at work in one of my web sites in Figure 10-5.
You can also get complete shopping cart software from PayPal.

There are other, similar options, such as Google Checkout, http://checkout
.google.com. You can even set up whole storefronts online with Yahoo stores:
http://smallbusiness.yahoo.com/ecommerce/.

MEMO

You can see the one problem I have with PayPal credit-card handling in Figure 10-5—PayPal doesn't automatically return the customers to your site (or at least, I've been unable to make it do so). The users have to click a button to get back to your site after they complete the transaction. That's an issue if you deliver to the customers what they've bought right after the transaction, such as a link to an e-book—some customers won't remember to click the Return To Merchant button.

Want to sell digital products, such as e-books? Check out ClickBank, shown in Figure 10-6, at www.clickbank.com/index.html, which has an affiliate system to help give you exposure.

And that completes this book! All that's needed now is to go out, put all this technology to work, and start reaping those profits!

Figure 10-5   Creating a Buy Now button

Figure 10-6   ClickBank

Index

255